SCIENTIFIC AMERICAN™
CUTTING-EDGE SCIENCE™

Tackling Cancer

New York

616.994
TAC

Published in 2007 by The Rosen Publishing Group, Inc.
29 East 21st Street, New York, NY 10010

The articles in this book first appeared in the pages of *Scientific American*, as follows: "Untangling the Roots of Cancer" by W. Wayt Gibbs, October 2004; "Vessels of Death or Life" by Rakesh K. Jain and Peter F. Carmeliet, December 2001; "The Long Arm of the Immune System" by Jacques Banchereau, November 2002; "New Light on Medicine" by Nick Lane, January 2003; "Tumor-Busting Viruses" by Dirk M. Nettelbeck and David T. Curiel, October 2003; "Hormone Hysteria" by Dennis Watkins, October 2003; "Skeptic: What's the Harm?" by Michael Shermer, December 2003; "Quiet Celebrity: Interview with Judah Folkman" by Sergio Pistoi and Chiara Palmerini, November 2002; "Profile: Peter H. Duesberg, Dissident or Don Quixote?" by W. Wayt Gibbs, August 2001.

First Edition

Library of Congress Cataloging-in-Publication Data

Tackling cancer.
    p. cm.—(Scientific American cutting-edge science)
Includes index.
ISBN-13: 978-1-4042-0987-9
ISBN-10: 1-4042-0987-5 (library binding)
1. Cancer. I. Scientific American.
RC262.T32 2007
616.99'4—dc22

                       2006024272

Manufactured in the United States of America

On the cover: In virotherapy, scientists are researching and testing the genetic engineering of viruses, such as these adenoviruses, to selectively infect and kill cancer cells, while leaving healthy cells untouched.

Illustration credits: Cover (foreground), p. 74 Terese Winslow; cover (background), p. 42 Jeff Johnson; p. 59 Slim Films; pp. 64–66 Hybrid Medical Animation; pp. 68–69 compiled by Tariq Malik; p. 110 Johnny Johnson/Source: Institute for Scientific Information *Web of Science*.

Contents

I. "Untangling the Roots of Cancer"

by W. Wayt Gibbs

Recent evidence challenges long-held theories of how cells turn malignant—and suggests new ways to stop tumors before they spread

What causes cancer? Tobacco smoke, most people would say. Probably too much alcohol, sunshine or grilled meat; infection with cervical papillomaviruses; asbestos. All have strong links to cancer, certainly. But they cannot be root causes. Much of the population is exposed to these carcinogens, yet only a tiny minority suffers dangerous tumors as a consequence. A cause, by definition, leads invariably to its effect. The immediate cause of cancer must be some combination of insults and accidents that induces normal cells in a healthy human body to turn malignant, growing like weeds and sprouting in unnatural places.

At this level, the cause of cancer is not entirely a mystery. In fact, a decade ago many geneticists were confident that science was homing in on a final answer: cancer is the result of cumulative mutations that alter specific locations in a cell's DNA and thus change the particular proteins encoded by cancer-related genes at those spots. The mutations affect two kinds of cancer genes. The first are called tumor suppressors. They normally restrain cells' ability to divide, and mutations permanently disable the genes. The second variety,

4

known as oncogenes, stimulate growth—in other words, cell division. Mutations lock oncogenes into an active state. Some researchers still take it as axiomatic that such growth-promoting changes to a small number of cancer genes are the initial event and root cause of every human cancer.

Others, however, including a few very prominent oncologists, are increasingly challenging that theory. No one questions that cancer is ultimately a disease of the DNA. But as biologists trace tumors to their roots, they have discovered many other abnormalities at work inside the nuclei of cells that, though not yet cancerous, are headed that way. Whole chromosomes, each containing 1,000 or more genes, are often lost or duplicated in their entirety. Pieces of chromosomes are frequently scrambled, truncated or fused together. Chemical additions to the DNA, or to the histone proteins around which it coils, somehow silence important genes—but in a reversible process quite different from mutation.

The accumulating evidence has spawned at least three hypotheses that compete with the standard dogma to explain what changes come first and which aberrations matter most in the transformation of a cell and its descendants from well-behaved tissue to invasive tumor. The challengers dispute the dominant view of the disease as the product of a defined genetic state. They argue that it is more useful to think of cancer as the consequence of a chaotic process, a combination of Murphy's Law and Darwin's Law: anything that can go wrong will, and in a competitive environment, the best adapted survive and prosper.

Despite that shared underlying principle, the new theories make different predictions about what kind of treatments will work best. Some suggest that many cancers could be prevented altogether by better screening, changes in diet, and new drugs—or even by old drugs, such as aspirin. Other theories cast doubt on that hope.

Marks of Malignancy

A WORKABLE THEORY of cancer has to explain both why it is predominantly a disease of old age and why we do not all die from it. A 70-year-old is roughly 100 times as likely to be diagnosed with a malignancy as a 19-year-old is. Yet most people make it to old age without getting cancer.

Biologists estimate that more than 10 million billion cells must cooperate to keep a human being healthy over the course of an 80-year life span. If any one of those myriad cells could give rise to a tumor, why is it that less than half the population will ever contract a cancer that is serious enough to catch a doctor's attention?

One explanation is that a cell must acquire several extraordinary skills to be malignant. "Five or six different regulatory systems must be perturbed in order for a normal cell to grow as a cancer," asserts Robert A. Weinberg of the Whitehead Institute at the Massachusetts Institute of Technology. In a November

2002 review paper, he and William C. Hahn of the Dana-Farber Cancer Institute in Boston argued that all life-threatening cancers manifest at least six special abilities, or "superpowers." (Although Weinberg is one of the founding proponents of the standard paradigm, even those who challenge that theory tend to agree with this view.)

For example, cancer cells continue dividing in situations in which normal cells would quietly wait for a special chemical signal—say, from an injured neighbor. Somehow they counterfeit these pro-growth messages. Conversely, tumor cells must ignore "stop dividing" commands that are sent out by the adjacent tissues they squeeze and by their own internal aging mechanisms.

All cancerous cells have serious problems of some sort with their DNA, and as they double again and again, many cells in the resulting colony end up far from the blood vessels that supply oxygen and nutrients.

Overview/How Cancer Arises

- Cancer is a genetic disease. Alterations to the DNA inside cells can endow cells with morbid "superpowers," such as the ability to grow anywhere and to continue dividing indefinitely.
- Most cancer researchers have long focused on mutations to a relatively small set of cancer-related genes as the decisive events in the transformation of healthy cells to malignant tumors.
- Recently, however, other theories have emerged to challenge this view. One hypothesizes that a breakdown in DNA duplication or repair leads to many thousands of random mutations in cells. Another suggests that damage to a few "master" genes mangles the chromosomes, which then become dangerous. A third challenger proposes that abnormal numbers of chromosomes in a cell may be the first milestone on the road to cancer.

Such stresses trigger autodestruct mechanisms in healthy cells. Tumor cells find some way to avoid this kind of suicide. Then they have to persuade nearby blood vessels to build the infrastructure they need to thrive.

A fifth superpower that almost all cancers acquire is immortality. A culture of normal human cells stops dividing after 50 to 70 generations. That is more than enough doublings to sustain a person through even a century of healthy life. But the great majority of cells in tumors quickly die of their genetic defects, so those that survive must reproduce indefinitely if the tumor is to grow. The survivors do so in part by manipulating their telomeres, gene-free complexes of DNA and protein that protect the ends of each chromosome.

Tumors that develop these five faculties are trouble, but they are probably not deadly. It is the sixth property, the ability to invade nearby tissue and then metastasize to distant parts of the body, that gives cancer its lethal character. Local invasions can usually be removed surgically. But nine of every 10 deaths from the disease are the result of metastases.

Only an elite few cells in a tumor seem to acquire this ability to detach from the initial mass, float through the circulatory system and start a new colony in a different organ from the one that gave birth to them. Unfortunately, by the time cancers are discovered, many have already metastasized—including, in the U.S., 72 percent of lung cancers, 57 percent of colorectal, and 34 percent of breast cancers. By then the prognosis is frequently grim.

The Order of Disorder

DOCTORS COULD CATCH incipient tumors sooner if scientists could trace the steps that cells take down the road to cancer after the initial assault to their DNA by

Six Diabolical Superpowers of Cancer

1. Growth even in the absence of normal "go" signals
   Most normal cells wait for an external message before dividing. Cancer cells often counterfeit their own pro-growth messages.

2. Growth despite "stop" commands issued by neighboring cells
   As the tumor expands, it squeezes adjacent tissue, which sends out chemical messages that would normally bring cell division to a halt. Malignant cells ignore the commands.

3. Evasion of built-in autodestruct mechanisms
   In healthy cells, genetic damage above a critical level usually activates a suicide program. Cancerous cells bypass this mechanism, although agents of the immune system can sometimes successfully order the cancer cells to self-destruct.

4. Ability to stimulate blood vessel construction
   Tumors need oxygen and nutrients to survive. They obtain them by co-opting nearby blood vessels to form new branches that run throughout the growing mass.

5. Effective immortality
   Healthy cells can divide no more than 70 times. Malignant cells need more than that to make tumors. So they work around systems—such as the telomeres at the end of chromosomes—that enforce the reproductive limit.

6. Power to invade other tissues and spread to other organs
   Cancers usually become life-threatening only after they somehow disable the cellular circuitry that confines them to a specific part of the particular organ in which they arose. New growths appear and eventually interfere with vital systems.

a carcinogen or some random biochemical mishap. Researchers broadly agree on the traits of the diseased cells that emerge from the journey. It is the propelling force and the order of each milestone that are under active debate.

The dominant paradigm has been that tumors grow in spurts of mutation and expansion. Genetic damage to a cell deletes or disrupts a tumor suppressor gene—*RB*, *p53* and *APC* are among the best known—thereby suppressing proteins that normally ensure the integrity of the genome and cell division. Alternatively, a mutation may increase the activity of an oncogene—such as *BRAF*, *c-fos* or *c-erbb3*—whose proteins then stimulate the cell to reproduce.

Changes to cancer genes endow the cell with one or more superpowers, allowing it to outbreed its neighbors. The cell passes abnormalities in its DNA sequence on to its descendants, which become a kind of clone army that grows to the limits of its capacity. Eventually another random mutation to a cancer gene knocks down another obstacle, initiating another burst of growth.

Cells normally have two copies of every chromosome—one from the mother, the other from the father—and thus two copies, or alleles, of every gene. (In males, the single X and Y chromosomes are notable exceptions.) A mutation to just one allele is enough to activate an oncogene permanently. But it takes two hits to knock out both alleles of a tumor suppressor gene. Four to 10 mutations in the right genes can transform any cell. Or so the theory goes.

The mutant-gene paradigm gained almost universal acceptance because it explained very well what scientists saw in their experiments on genetically engineered mice and human cell cultures. But new technologies now allow researchers to study the genomes of cancerous and precancerous cells taken directly from people. Many recent observations seem to contradict the idea that mutations to a few specific genes lie at the root of all cancers.

Unexplained Phenomena

IN APRIL 2003, for example, Muhammad Al-Hajj of the University of Michigan at Ann Arbor and his colleagues reported that they had identified distinguishing marks for a rare subset of cells within human breast cancers that can form new tumors. As few as 100 cells of this type quickly spawned disease when injected into mice lacking an immune system. Tens of thousands of other cells, harvested from the same nine breast malignancies but lacking the telltale marks, failed to do so. "This is the first tumor-initiating cell anyone has isolated for solid tumors," says John E. Dick, a biologist at the University of Toronto who has identified similar cells for leukemia.

The tantalizing implication, Dick says, is that just a small fraction of the cells in a tumor are responsible for its growth and metastasis. If that is shown to be true for humans as well as mice, it could pose a problem for the mutant-gene theory of cancer. If mutations, which are copied from a cell to its progeny, give tumor cells their powers, then shouldn't all clones in the army be equally powerful?

In fact, most tumors are not masses of identical clones. On the contrary, closer examination has revealed amazing genetic diversity among their cells, some of which are so different from normal human cells (and from one another) that they might fairly be called new species.

A few cancer-related genes, such as *p53*, do seem to be mutated in the majority of tumors. But many other cancer genes are changed in only a small fraction of cancer types, a minority of patients, or a sprinkling of cells within a tumor. David Sidransky of the Johns Hopkins University School of Medicine and his co-workers tested DNA from 476 tumors of various kinds. They reported in April 2003 that the oncogene *BRAF* was altered in two thirds of papillary thyroid cancers but not in any of several other kinds of thyroid cancers.

Moreover, some of the most commonly altered cancer genes have oddly inconsistent effects. Bert E. Vogelstein's group at Johns Hopkins found that the much studied oncogenes *c-fos* and *c-erbb3* are curiously less active in tumors than they are in nearby normal tissues. The tumor suppressor gene *RB* was recently shown to be hyperactive—not disabled—in some colon cancers, and, perversely, it appears to protect those tumors from their autodestruct mechanisms.

The "two hit" hypothesis—that both alleles of a tumor suppressor gene must be deactivated—has also been upended by the discovery of a phenomenon called haploinsufficiency. In some cancers, tumor suppressors are not mutated at all. Their output is simply reduced, and that seems to be enough to push cells toward malignancy. This effect has now been seen for more than a dozen tumor suppressor genes. Searching for the mere presence or absence of a gene's protein is too simplistic. Dosage matters.

Beyond Mutation

RESEARCHERS ARE NOW looking more closely at other phenomena that could dramatically alter the dosage of a protein in a cell. Candidates include the loss or gain of a chromosome (or part of one) containing the gene; changes in the concentration of other proteins that regulate how the gene is transcribed from DNA to RNA and translated into a protein; even so-called epigenetic phenomena that alter gene activity by reversible means. All these changes are nearly ubiquitous in established cancers.

"If you look at most solid tumors in adults, it looks like someone set off a bomb in the nucleus," Hahn says. "In most cells, there are big pieces of chromosomes hooked together and duplications or losses of whole chromosomes."

Scientists have yet to settle on a term for the suite of chromosomal aberrations seen in cancer. The word "aneuploidy" once referred to an abnormal number of chromosomes. But more recently, it has been used in a broader sense that encompasses chromosomes with truncations, extensions or swapped segments.

Almost a century ago German biologist Theodor Boveri noticed the strange imbalance in cancer cells between the numbers of maternal versus paternal chromosomes. He even suggested that aneuploid cells might cause the disease. But scientists could find no recurrent pattern to the chromosomal chaos—indeed, the genome of a typical cancer cell is not merely aneuploid but is unstable as well, changing every few generations. So Boveri's idea was dropped as the search for oncogenes started to bear fruit. The aneuploidy and massive genomic instability inside tumor cells were dismissed as side effects of cancer, not prerequisites.

But the oncogene/tumor suppressor gene hypothesis has also failed, despite two decades of effort, to identify a particular set of gene mutations that occurs in every instance of any of the most common and deadly kinds of human cancer. The list of cancer-related mutations has grown to more than 100 oncogenes and 15 tumor suppressor genes. "The rate at which these molecular markers are being identified continues to increase rapidly," lamented Weinberg and Hahn in their 2002 review. "As a consequence," they added, "it remains possible that each tumor is unique" in the pattern of its genetic disarray.

Hahn reflected on this possibility in his Boston office in January 2003. Along with Weinberg, he has pioneered the construction of artificial tumors using mutant cancer genes. But he acknowledged that they cannot be the whole story. "The question is which comes first," he said. "Mutations or aneuploidy?"

There are at least three competing answers. Let us call them the modified dogma, the early instability theory and the all-aneuploidy theory. Encouragingly, the theories seem to be converging as they bend to accommodate new experimental results.

The modified form of the standard dogma revives an idea proposed in 1974 by Lawrence A. Loeb, now at the University of Washington. He and others have estimated that random mutation will affect just one gene in any given cell over a lifetime. Something—a carcinogen, reactive oxidants, or perhaps a malfunction in the cell's DNA duplication and repair machinery— must dramatically accelerate the mutation rate, Loeb argues. "I think that is probably right," Hahn concurs. Otherwise, he says, "cells wouldn't accumulate a sufficient number of mutations to form a tumor."

Loeb believes that "early during the genesis of cancer there are enormous numbers of random mutations—10,000 to 100,000 per cell." Evidence for the theory is still slim, he acknowledges. Counting random mutations is hard; scientists must compare the genomes of individual cells letter by letter. Advances in biotechnology have only recently made that feasible.

The modified dogma thus adds a prologue to the accepted life history of cancer. But the most important are still mutations to genes that serve to increase the reproductive success of cells. Mangled and ever changing chromosomes are but fortuitous by-products.

Unstable from the Outset

CRISTOPH LENGAUER and Vogelstein of Johns Hopkins, both well-known colon cancer specialists, have proposed an alternative theory in which chromosomal instability can occur early on. The genetic flux then combines forces with natural selection to produce a benign growth that may later be converted to an invasive malignancy and life-threatening metastases.

In their hypothesis, there are several "master" genes whose function is critical for a cell to reproduce correctly. If as few as one of these genes is disabled, either by mutation or epigenetically, the cell stumbles each time it attempts cell division, muddling some of the chromosomes into an aneuploid state. One result is to increase 100,000-fold the rate at which cells randomly lose one of the two alleles of their genes. For a tumor suppressor gene, a lost allele may effectively put the gene out of commission, either because the remaining copy is already mutated or because of the haploinsufficiency effect. Lengauer and Vogelstein still assume that some cancer genes must be altered before a malignancy can erupt.

In December 2002, together with Martin A. Nowak and Natalia L. Komarova of the Institute for Advanced Study in Princeton, N.J., Lengauer and Vogelstein published a mathematical analysis that applied this theory to nonhereditary colon cancer. Even if there are as few as half a dozen master genes in the human genome, they calculated, it is very likely that a master gene will be disabled before a particular cancer gene is hit.

Calculations are fine, but only empirical evidence is persuasive. Some recent studies do support the early instability theory. In 2000 Lengauer's laboratory examined colon adenomas—benign polyps that occasionally turn malignant—and observed that more than 90 percent had extra or missing pieces of at least one chromosome. More than half had lost the long arm of chromosome 5, home to the *APC* tumor suppressor gene, long implicated in the formation of colon cancer. Other researchers have discovered similarly aberrant chromosomes in precancerous growths taken from the stomach, esophagus and breast.

The early instability theory still has some loose ends, however. How can cells with shifty chromosomes outcompete their stable counterparts? Under normal conditions, they probably do not, suggests immunologist Jarle Breivik of the University of Oslo. But in a "war zone," where a carcinogen or other stressor is continually inflicting damage to cells, normal cells stop dividing until they have completed repairs to their

DNA. Genetically unstable cells get that way because their DNA repair systems are already broken. So they simply ignore the damage, keep on proliferating, and thus pull ahead, Breivik hypothesizes.

He cites an experiment in which Lengauer and his colleagues exposed human cell lines to toxic levels of a carcinogen in broiled meat. Only a few cells developed resistance and survived. All were genetically unstable before exposure to the toxin.

But what jumbles the chromosomes in the first place? No genes have yet been conclusively identified as master genes, although several strong suspects have surfaced. German A. Pihan of the University of Massachusetts Medical School and his co-workers may have uncovered a clue in a March 2003 study of 116 premalignant tumors caught before they had invaded neighboring tissues of the cervix, prostate and breast. Thirty to 72 percent of the growths contained defective centrosomes, structures that appear during cell division to help separate the duplicated chromosomes from the originals. Most of those cells were aneuploid. Scientists are still working out the genes that control centrosome formation and function; any of them might be a master gene.

Aneuploidy All the Way Down

ON THE OTHER HAND, maybe cells can become malignant even before any master genes, oncogenes or tumor suppressor genes are mutated. Peter H. Duesberg and

Ruhong Li of the University of California at Berkeley have put forth a third theory: nearly all cancer cells are aneuploid because they start that way. Lots of things can interfere with a dividing cell so that one of its daughter cells is cheated of its normal complement of 46 chromosomes and the other daughter is endowed with a bonus. Asbestos fibers, Duesberg notes, can physically disrupt the process.

Most aneuploid cells are stillborn or growth-retarded. But in the rare survivor, he suggests, the dosage of thousands of genes is altered. That corrupts teams of enzymes that synthesize and maintain DNA. Breaks appear in the double helix, destabilizing the genome further. "The more aneuploid the cell is, the more unstable it is, and the more likely it will produce new combinations of chromosomes that will allow it to grow anywhere," Duesberg explains.

Unlike the three other theories, the all-aneuploidy hypothesis predicts that the emergence and progress of a tumor are more closely connected to the assortment of chromosomes in its cells than to the mutations in the genes on those chromosomes. Some observations do seem to corroborate the idea.

In May 2003, for instance, Duesberg and scientists at the University of Heidelberg reported on experiments with normal and aneuploid hamster embryos. The more the cells deviated from the correct number of chromosomes, the faster aberrations accumulated in their chromosomes. Genomic instability rose exponentially with greater aneuploidy.

Thomas Ried, chief of cancer genomics at the National Cancer Institute, has obtained supporting evidence in humans with cervical and colorectal cancers. "Unequivocally, there are recurrent patterns of genomic imbalances," Ried avers. "Every single case of [nonhereditary] colorectal cancer, for example, has gains of chromosomes 7, 8, 13 or 20 or a loss of 18. In cervical cancer, aneuploidy of chromosome 3 happens very early, and those cells seem to have a selective advantage." Ried finds the average number of abnormal chromosomes increasing gradually from 0.2 in a normal cell to 12 in the cells of metastatic colon tumors.

"So I think Duesberg is right that aneuploidy can be the first genetic aberration in cancer cells," Ried says. "But he also argues that no gene mutations are required. This is simply not true."

Stopping Cancer at Its Roots

NEITHER THE standard dogma nor any of the new theories can explain the 100-odd diseases we call cancer as variations of a single principle. And all the theories will need to be expanded to incorporate the role of epigenetic phenomena.

It is important to determine which of the ideas is more correct than the others, because they each make different predictions about the kinds of therapy that will succeed. In the standard view, tumors are in effect addicted to the proteins produced by oncogenes and are poisoned by tumor suppressor proteins. Medicines should therefore be designed to break the addiction or supply the poison. Indeed, this strategy is exploited by some newer drugs, such as Gleevec (for rare forms of leukemia and stomach cancer) and Herceptin (for one variety of advanced breast cancer).

But all existing therapies fail in some patients because their tumors evolve into a resistant strain. Loeb fears that there may be no easy way around that problem. "If I am right, then within any given tumor, which contains roughly 100 million cells, there will be cells with random mutations that protect them from any treatment you can conceive," Loeb says. "So the best you can hope for is to delay the tumor's growth. You are not going to cure it."

For the elderly—who, after all, are the main victims of cancer—a sufficient delay may be as good as a cure. And even better than slowing the growth of a tumor would be to delay its formation in the first place. If Lengauer and other adherents of the early instability theory succeed in identifying master genes, then it should also be possible to make drugs that protect or restore their function. Lengauer says his group has already licensed cell lines to the pharmaceutical industry to use in drug screening.

Screening of a different kind may be the best approach if the all-aneuploidy theory is correct. There is no known means of selectively killing cells with abnormal chromosomes. But a biopsy that turns up a surfeit of aneuploid cells might warrant careful monitoring or even preventive surgery in certain cases. And Duesberg suggests that foods, drugs and chemicals should be tested to identify compounds that cause aneuploidy.

One day science will produce a definitive answer to the question of what causes cancer. It will probably be a very complicated answer, and it may force us to shift our hope from drugs that cure the disease to medicines that prevent it. Even without a clear understanding of why, doctors have discovered that a daily baby aspirin seems to prevent colon adenomas in some adults. The effect is small. But it is a step from chemotherapy toward a better alternative: chemoprevention.

The Author

W. WAYT GIBBS is senior writer for *Scientific American*.

More to Explore

Chromosome Segregation and Cancer: Cutting through the Mystery. Prasad V. Jallepalli and Cristoph Lengauer in *Nature Reviews Cancer*, Vol. 1, No. 2, pages 109–117; November 2001.

Rules for Making Human Tumor Cells. William C. Hahn and Robert A. Weinberg in *New England Journal of Medicine*, Vol. 347, No. 20, pages 1593–1603; November 14, 2002.

Multiple Mutations and Cancer. Lawrence A. Loeb, Keith R. Loeb and Jon P. Anderson in *Proceedings of the National Academy of Sciences USA*, Vol. 100, No. 3, pages 776–781; February 4, 2003.

"Vessels of
2. Death or Life"

by Rakesh K. Jain and Peter F. Carmeliet

Angiogenesis—the formation of new blood vessels—might one day be manipulated to treat disorders from cancer to heart disease. First-generation drugs are now in the final phase of human testing

They snake through our bodies, literally conveying our life's blood, their courses visible through our skin only as faint bluish tracks or ropy cords. We hardly give them a thought until we cut ourselves or visit a clinic to donate blood. But blood vessels play surprisingly central roles in many serious chronic disorders. New growth of the body's smallest vessels, for instance, enables cancers to enlarge and spread and contributes to the blindness that can accompany diabetes. Conversely, lack of small vessel, or capillary, production can contribute to other ills, such as tissue death in cardiac muscle after a heart attack. Accordingly, we and other scientists are working to understand the mechanisms that underlie abnormal vessel growth. This effort will help us develop and optimize drugs that block vessel growth—or improve vessel function.

The study of small vessel growth—a phenomenon referred to generally as angiogenesis—has such potential for providing new therapies that it has been the subject of countless news stories and has received enthusiastic interest from the pharmaceutical and biotechnology industries. Indeed, dozens of companies are now pursuing angiogenesis-related therapies, and approximately 20 compounds that either induce or block vessel formation are being tested in humans. Although such drugs can potentially treat a broad range of disorders, many of the compounds now under investigation inhibit angiogenesis and target cancer. We will therefore focus the bulk of our discussion on those agents. Intriguingly, animal tests show that inhibitors of vessel growth can boost the effectiveness of traditional cancer treatments (chemotherapy and radiation). Preliminary studies also hint that the agents might one day be delivered as a preventive measure to block malignancies from arising in the first place in people at risk for cancer.

Results from the first human tests of several compounds that block blood vessel growth were announced earlier this year. Some observers were disappointed because few of the patients, who had cancer, showed improvement. But those tests were designed solely to assess whether the compounds are safe and nontoxic, which they appear to be. Human tests of efficacy are under way and will be a much better judge of whether angiogenesis inhibitors can live up to their very great promise.

The Genesis of Angiogenesis

THE TERM "angiogenesis" technically refers to the branching and extension of existing capillaries, whose walls consist of just one layer of so-called endothelial cells. In its normal guise, angiogenesis helps to repair injured tissues. In females it also builds the lining of the uterus each month before menstruation and forms the placenta after fertilization. The development of blood vessels is governed by a balance of naturally occurring proangiogenic and antiangiogenic factors. Angiogenesis is switched on by growth factors such as vascular endothelial growth factor (VEGF) and is turned off by inhibitors such as thrombospondin. When the regulation of this balance is disturbed, as occurs during tumor growth, vessels form at inappropriate times and places.

Cancer researchers became interested in angiogenesis factors in 1968, when the first hints emerged that tumors might release such substances to foster their own progression. Two independent research teams— Melvin Greenblatt of the University of Southern California, working with Phillipe Shubik of the University of Chicago, and Robert L. Ehrmann and

Overview/Angiogenesis

- More than 20 compounds that manipulate angiogenesis—either by stimulating new blood vessel growth or by blocking it—are now in human tests against a range of disorders, from cancer to heart disease.
- Angiogenesis inhibitors are generally safe and less toxic than chemotherapeutic drugs, but they are unlikely to treat cancer effectively on their own. Instead physicians will probably use angiogenesis inhibitors in conjunction with standard cancer treatments such as surgery, chemotherapy and radiation.
- The blood vessels of tumors are abnormal. Surprisingly, angiogenesis inhibitors appear to "normalize" tumor vessels before they kill them. This normalization can help anticancer agents reach tumors more effectively.

Mogens Knoth of Harvard Medical School—showed that burgeoning tumors release a then unidentified substance that induces existing blood vessels to grow into them. Such proliferation promotes tumor growth because it ensures a rich supply of blood loaded with oxygen and nutrients. In 1971 Judah Folkman of Harvard proposed that interfering with this factor might be a way to kill tumors, by starving them of a blood supply. What is more, Folkman later posited that blocking the factor could slow cancer's spread, a process called metastasis, because cancer cells must enter blood vessels to travel to other parts of the body.

Nipping New Blood Vessels in the Bud

CURRENT TESTS of angiogenesis inhibitors against cancer employ several different strategies. Chief among these is interfering with the action of VEGF. This molecule, which was initially named vascular permeability factor when it was discovered in 1983 by Harold F. Dvorak and his colleagues at Harvard, appears to be the most prevalent proangiogenic factor identified to date. Scientists gained a tool for better understanding the function of VEGF in 1989, when Napoleone Ferrara of Genentech and his co-workers isolated the gene encoding the molecule. In 1996 groups led by Ferrara and one of us (Carmeliet) independently demonstrated the critical role of VEGF in vessel formation by generating mice that lacked one of the normal two copies of the VEGF gene. The mice, which made half the usual amount of VEGF, died in the womb from insufficient and abnormally organized blood vessels.

Researchers are exploring a number of ways to neutralize VEGF's angiogenic activity in patients. These include immune system proteins called antibodies that can bind specifically to and disable VEGF; soluble forms of the cellular receptors for VEGF, to act as decoys that sop up the growth factor before it can bind to cells; and small molecules that can enter cells and block the growth messages that VEGF sends into an endothelial cell's interior after binding to receptors at the surface. The compounds under study also include factors, such as interferons, that decrease the production of VEGF and substances, such as so-called metalloproteinase inhibitors, that block the release of VEGF from storage depots in the extracellular matrix, the "glue" that binds cells together to create tissues.

Although halving the amount of VEGF is lethal to mouse embryos, wiping out cancers in humans with such therapies will probably require the complete neutralization of all the VEGF protein present in a tumor, and that might be difficult to do. VEGF is a potent agent, and trace amounts could protect the endothelial cells from death. But even after all the VEGF is neutralized, a tumor could rely on other proangiogenic factors, such as basic fibroblast growth factor or interleukin-8.

Another widely studied approach for inhibiting angiogenesis in cancer patients is administering or increasing the natural production of antiangiogenic factors. The idea for this therapy emerged when Folkman learned that Noel Bouck of Northwestern University had identified a naturally occurring inhibitor—thrombospondin—in 1989. Surgeons already knew that removing a patient's primary tumor in some cases accelerated the growth of other, smaller tumors—almost as if the primary tumor had secreted something that kept the smaller tumors in check. They have never questioned the necessity of removing the primary tumor in most cases, because such tumors often obstruct the normal functions of organs and tissues, and leaving them in place would provide a source of cancerous cells for yet more metastases. But discovery of a natural angiogenesis inhibitor suggested to Folkman that the primary tumor's secretions might be harnessed as cancer drugs to suppress the growth of both primary and small metastases.

With this concept in mind, Folkman and his colleagues discovered two more of these naturally occurring antiangiogenic substances—angiostatin and endostatin—in 1994 and 1997, respectively. These inhibitors have received a great deal of attention. This is in part because of studies by Folkman's group showing that they can eradicate tumors in mice. A front-page story heralding such successes in 1998 in the *New York Times* increased the visibility of the entire field of angiogenesis.

Clinical trials of angiostatin and endostatin are currently in early stages (experiments involving small

Therapeutic Angiogenesis

When making more blood vessels is good for the body

It's easy to understand how restricting the growth of new blood vessels could help kill tumors, but fostering vessel growth—a strategy termed therapeutic angiogenesis—could be useful against other disorders.

Researchers around the world are now evaluating whether the angiogenic substances they are trying to block to treat cancer might help heart attack patients—or those at risk for heart attack—grow new blood vessels in the heart. Those factors might also be used to treat people with vascular disorders in their feet and legs.

A heart attack, properly called a myocardial infarction, occurs when a blood clot forms in one of the arteries that feeds the heart muscle, preventing part of the heart from receiving oxygen and nutrients, a condition known as ischemia. Unless the clot is dissolved or dislodged rapidly, the patch of heart muscle can die. In addition, many diabetics suffer from a lack of circulation in their extremities caused by occluded blood vessels; some require amputations.

Therapeutic angiogenesis can involve directly administering a vessel growth–promoting substance, such as vascular endothelial growth factor (VEGF). It can also be accomplished using gene therapy, administering to a patient genetically engineered viruses, cells or pieces of DNA that carry the gene encoding VEGF or another angiogenic factor.

Therapeutic angiogenesis with VEGF or fibroblast growth factor (FGF) has been explored for the past 10 years. In 1991 scientists led by Stephen H. Epstein of the National Institutes of Health studied the effects of FGF on the heart vessels of animals. A year later Paul Friedmann and his co-workers at Baystate Medical Center in Springfield, Mass., showed that FGF injections could prompt angiogenesis in the hind limbs of rabbits. In the mid-1990s several groups—including those led by Epstein, Michael Simons of Harvard Medical School, Jeffrey M. Isner of St. Elizabeth's Medical Center in Boston and Ronald G. Crystal of Cornell University Medical School in New York City—demonstrated that therapy involving angiogenic factors or the genes that encode them could stimulate angiogenesis in the hearts and limbs of animals.

Clinical trials aimed at evaluating the safety and efficacy of angiogenic factors in patients are now under way. Carmeliet and others are also testing the therapeutic potential of other promising molecules, such as placental growth factor, a relative of VEGF. Creating functional blood vessels appears to be a formidable challenge, however. Researchers are trying to find the best combinations of such proangiogenic agents as well as the optimal dose, administration schedule and delivery route for the drugs. They are also evaluating whether transplants of endothelial stem cells—the precursors of the endothelial cells that make up blood vessels—can augment the regeneration of blood vessels. Such stem cells can be isolated from the bone marrow of adults.

But potential risks accompany the promise of proangiogenic therapy. Therapeutic angiogenesis could increase a patient's risk of cancer by allowing tiny tumors that had been dormant in the body to gain a blood supply and grow. In addition, because the atherosclerotic plaques that underlie heart disease require their own blood supply as they become larger, therapeutic angiogenesis could backfire as a treatment for cardiac disease by stimulating the growth of plaques that had caused the individual's heart attack in the first place.

Human studies to evaluate the likelihood of these dire scenarios have only recently begun. We hope one day to be able to use genetic tests to evaluate a patient's natural balance of proangiogenic and antiangiogenic factors before beginning to treat them with proangiogenic drugs. This information might also help us understand whether myocardial ischemia results from the insufficient production of angiogenic factors or from the excess production of angiogenic inhibitors. The results will undoubtedly aid in the development of more directed strategies for therapeutic angiogenesis.
—R. K. J. and P. F. C.

numbers of patients to evaluate a potential drug's safety). Preliminary results reported at this year's American Society of Clinical Oncology conference, which were alluded to earlier, indicate that endostatin is safe and causes no side effects. We await the outcome of the various clinical trials of these and other angiogenesis inhibitors in the coming years.

Going after Established Blood Vessels

THE TWO APPROACHES described thus far interfere with the formation of new blood vessels. But what about preexisting vessels in a tumor? Is it possible to target those without disrupting the established vessels in healthy tissues and organs (an approach termed anti-vascular therapy)?

Luckily, it turns out that the blood vessels of tumors are abnormal. Not only are they structurally disorganized, tortuous, dilated and leaky, but the cells that compose them display certain molecules on their surfaces from a class known as integrins that are absent or barely detectable in mature vessels. Biologists have recently produced small proteins, called RGD peptides, that preferentially recognize the integrins on tumor vessels. These peptides can be linked to cell-killing drugs to target such therapeutic agents to tumors without damaging other tissues. They could also be used to clog the vessels that feed the tumor, by delivering molecules that cause blood clots to form.

But it might not be so easy for any drug to zero in on all a given tumor's blood vessels. The individual cells that make up even a single tumor vessel can vary widely. Studies in one of our labs (Jain's) have found that 15 percent of the blood vessels in human colon cancers are mosaic: some have a particular protein on their surfaces, whereas others do not. If the proteins targeted by new drugs turn out to differ from one tumor to the next or to vary within a tumor during the course of its growth or treatment, this heterogeneity will make it difficult to get therapies that target blood vessels to work on their own.

Combine and Conquer

MOST LIKELY, surgery or radiation—or both—will continue to be used to attempt to eliminate the original tumor. Today chemotherapy is often administered before or after such therapy to shrink tumors and mop up undetectable malignant cells remaining in the body. Antiangiogenic drugs could well be combined with any of the other approaches to improve the success rate.

Angiogenesis Inhibitors Nearing the Market

These potential therapies for cancer are in phase III testing, the last stage before Food and Drug Administration approval. Angiostatin and endostatin are in earlier phases of evaluation. Similar compounds are also in trials against the eye disease macular degeneration.

PRODUCT	DEVELOPER	DESCRIPTION	DISEASE TARGET
Avastin	Genentech	Monoclonal antibody that disables vascular endothelial growth factor (VEGF), a promoter of angiogenesis	Breast and colorectal cancer
BMS275291	Bristol-Myers Squibb	Synthetic compound having multiple effects	Nonsmall cell lung cancer
Interferon alpha	Roche, Schering	Protein that inhibits release of growth factors such as VEGF	Various tumors
Marimastat	British Biotech	Synthetic compound having multiple effects	Breast and prostate cancer
Neovastat	Aeterna	Naturally occurring inhibitor with a range of properties	Nonsmall cell lung and renal cancer
SU5416	Sugen	Synthetic compound that blocks the receptor for VEGF	Colorectal cancer
Thalidomide	Celgene	Organic molecule whose specific mechanism of action is unknown	Renal cancer and multiple myeloma

Following the pioneering studies of Beverly Teicher of Harvard in the 1990s, several groups have shown the benefits of such a combined approach. Recently Folkman, Robert Kerbel of the University of Toronto and Jain's group have found that combined therapy can produce long-term cures in mice.

Interestingly, antiangiogenic therapy appears to boost the effectiveness of traditional cancer treatments. This is surprising because chemotherapeutic agents depend on blood vessels to reach a tumor, and radiation kills only those cells that have an adequate supply of oxygen (it turns oxygen into toxic free radicals). Logic suggests that by compromising the blood supply of tumors, antiangiogenic therapy would interfere with the effectiveness of these standard treatments. But scientists have demonstrated that the delivery of chemotherapy—as well as nutrients and oxygen—improves during the course of some antiangiogenic therapies.

Indeed, researchers led by Jain have shown that antiangiogenic factors can "normalize" tumor vasculature before killing it by pruning excess, inefficient vessels while leaving efficient vessels temporarily intact. In studies of mice, the researchers found that angiogenesis inhibitors decreased the diameters of tumor blood vessels and made them less leaky, so they began to resemble normal vessels. If such studies pan out in humans, however, physicians will need to work out the optimal dosage and timing of administration.

As is true for many drugs, future generations of antiangiogenic agents are likely to be more effective than the first generation. To optimize future drugs, researchers will need to modify their investigation methods. Most preclinical studies, performed before a drug can be tested in people, are carried out on tumors that are artificially grown under the skin of animals such as mice. But few human tumors arise beneath the skin. To get a more realistic idea of whether a given cancer drug will work in people, researchers will need to study animals with spontaneously occurring tumors growing in more natural sites.

Another limitation of preclinical studies is that they are time-intensive and costly, so researchers usually halt them when tumors begin to shrink but before they can be sure a treatment being tested will actually eradicate the cancers. Because tumors can recur from even a very small number of surviving cancer cells, scientists should follow treated animals for longer periods to better determine the promise of new drug candidates. In addition, investigators tend to begin administering experimental drugs to animals before tumors are fully established, at a time when the cancers are vulnerable—possibly tilting the scales in the drug's favor. Animal tumors also tend to grow more quickly than those in people, and drugs that kill such fast-growing cancers might not be effective against slower-growing human tumors.

Researchers also need to study combinations of antiangiogenic drugs. Cancer cells are masters of evasion. Each tumor produces different combinations of angiogenic molecules that may vary or broaden as they grow. Administering an antiangiogenic drug that blocks only one molecule, such as VEGF, can simply prompt tumors to use another proangiogenic substance to attract a blood supply. In the end, optimal antiangiogenic therapy might consist of a cocktail of several angiogenesis inhibitors.

An Ounce of Prevention

IF ANGIOGENESIS INHIBITORS fulfill their early promise against cancer, patients will probably need to take them for a long time. The drugs might also be administered as cancer preventatives to people with a high risk of particular cancers—an approach initially suggested in 1976 by Pietro M. Gullino of the National Cancer Institute. Consequently, they must be shown to be safe over the long term. (The drug interferon, an indirect antiangiogenic agent, has been given for years with no side effects to pediatric patients with hemangiomas—benign blood vessel tumors.) The existing human trials will not address this question; they are designed to evaluate safety for just a few months. Animal studies hint that some antiangiogenic compounds might not be safe enough for the long-term administration required to prevent growth or relapse of cancer. Mice that have been genetically manipulated to reduce their production of VEGF can develop neurological defects after a prolonged period, for example, as shown in experiments by Carmeliet.

Insufficient angiogenesis can also impair the heart's recovery from ischemia, tissue starvation stemming from a poor supply of blood. During a heart attack, a blood clot lodges in an artery that supplies the heart muscle, killing a part of the organ. Indeed, researchers are testing agents that spur angiogenesis as treatments for ischemic heart disease. Accordingly, antiangiogenic cancer treatments might increase a patient's risk of ischemic heart disease. As with any therapy, then, physicians and patients will have to carefully weigh the risks and benefits of using angiogenesis inhibitors.

Nevertheless, the burgeoning understanding of angiogenesis has changed our thinking about how to attack cancer. Current treatment with radiation and chemotherapy halts many cancers, but too often the existing treatments bring about only a temporary symptom-free period before the tumor shows up again, spreads throughout the body and kills. Part of the problem is that physicians and pathologists lack reliable, sensitive, cheap and easy-to-use tests that can identify characteristics about each patient's cancer that indicate the best treatment strategy. Genetic analyses of tumors and patients promise to improve the accuracy of diagnoses as well as the efficacy and safety of treatments in the future, but we suspect that within the next 10 or 20 years, better visualization of abnormal vessel structure and function will help as well.

Antiangiogenic approaches have already shown benefit in patients with hemangiomas. As knowledge of tumor angiogenesis progresses, cancers may be detected through elevated levels of angiogenic molecules in the blood—long before clinical symptoms. Physicians may begin to examine patients regularly using molecular tests and new imaging techniques to determine an individual's profile of proangiogenic and antiangiogenic factors.

Based on such tests, doctors will be able to devise treatment plans that, along with other therapies, incorporate a mix of angiogenesis inhibitors appropriate for that individual's tumor. Tests that detect the presence of abnormal vessels will allow doctors to detect possible relapses at an early, potentially treatable stage. Perhaps, as safe oral antiangiogenic drugs are developed and become available, cancer patients will be able to take "a pill a day to keep the cancer away." If so, forms of cancer that are currently untreatable will be reduced to chronic health problems similar to hypertension or diabetes, and many more people will be able to live long, satisfying lives.

The Authors

RAKESH K. JAIN and *PETER F. CARMELIET* bring complementary backgrounds to the study of angiogenesis. Jain, who is now the Andrew Werk Cook Professor of Tumor Biology at Harvard Medical School and director of the Edwin L. Steele Laboratory at Massachusetts General Hospital, started his career as a chemical engineer. He held posts at Columbia University and at Carnegie Mellon University before joining Harvard in 1991. Carmeliet is a professor of medicine at the University of Leuven in Belgium, where he also serves as adjunct director of the Center for Transgene Technology and Gene Therapy at the Flanders Interuniversity Institute of Biotechnology. He received his M.D. from Leuven in 1984 and his Ph.D. from the same institution in 1989.

More to Explore

"An Address System in the Vasculature of Normal Tissues and Tumors." E. Ruoslahti and D. Rajotte in *Annual Review of Immunology*, Vol. 18, pages 813–827; 2000.

"Angiogenesis in Cancer and Other Diseases." P. Carmeliet and R. K. Jain in *Nature*, Vol. 407, pages 249–257; September 14, 2000.

"Angiogenesis." J. Folkman in *Harrison's Principles of Internal Medicine*. Fifteenth edition. Edited by E. Braunwald, A. S. Fauci, D. L. Kasper, S. L. Hauser, D. L. Longo and J. L. Jameson. McGraw-Hill, 2001.

The National Cancer Institute Web site provides updates on cancer trials that are using angiogenesis inhibitors: **www.cancertrials.nci.nih.gov**

"The Long Arm of
3. the Immune System"

by Jacques Banchereau

Dendritic cells catch invaders and tell the immune system when and how to respond. Vaccines depend on them, and scientists are even employing the cells to stir up immunity against cancer

They lie buried—their long, tentaclelike arms outstretched—in all the tissues of our bodies that interact with the environment. In the lining of our nose and lungs, lest we inhale the influenza virus in a crowded subway car. In our gastrointestinal tract, to alert our immune system if we swallow a dose of salmonella bacteria. And most important, in our skin, where they lie in wait as stealthy sentinels should microbes breach the leathery fortress of our epidermis.

They are dendritic cells, a class of white blood cells that encompasses some of the least understood but most fascinating actors in the immune system. Over the past several years, researchers have begun to unravel the mysteries of how dendritic cells educate the immune system about what belongs in the body and what is foreign and potentially dangerous. Intriguingly, they have found that dendritic cells initiate and control the overall immune response. For instance, the cells are crucial for establishing immunological "memory," which is the basis of all vaccines. Indeed, physicians, including those at a number of biotechnology companies, are taking advantage of the role that dendritic cells play in immunization by "vaccinating" cancer patients with dendritic cells loaded with bits of their own tumors to activate their immune system against their cancer. Dendritic cells are also responsible for the phenomenon of immune tolerance, the process through which the immune system learns not to attack other components of the body.

But dendritic cells can have a dark side. The human immunodeficiency virus (HIV) hitches a ride inside dendritic cells to travel to lymph nodes, where it infects and wipes out helper T cells, causing AIDS. And those cells that become active at the wrong time might give rise to autoimmune disorders such as lupus. In these cases, shutting down the activity of dendritic cells could lead to new therapies.

Rare and Precious

DENDRITIC CELLS are relatively scarce: they constitute only 0.2 percent of white blood cells in the blood and are present in even smaller proportions in tissues such as the skin. In part because of their rarity, their true function eluded scientists for nearly a century after they were first identified in 1868 by German anatomist Paul Langerhans, who mistook them for nerve endings in the skin.

In 1973 Ralph M. Steinman of the Rockefeller University rediscovered the cells in mouse spleens and recognized that they are part of the immune system. The cells were unusually potent in stimulating immunity in experimental animals. He renamed the cells "dendritic" because of their spiky arms, or dendrites, although the subset of dendritic cells that occur in the epidermis layer of the skin are still commonly called Langerhans cells.

For almost 20 years after the cells' rediscovery, researchers had to go through a painstakingly slow process to isolate them from fresh tissue for study. But

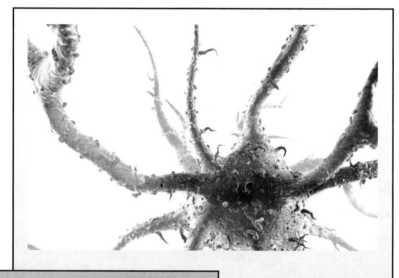

Overview/Dendritic Cells

- Dendritic cells—named for their long arms, or dendrites—exist in many tissues, particularly the skin and mucous membranes. They reel in invaders, chop them into pieces called antigens and display the antigens on their surfaces.
- Antigen-bearing dendritic cells travel to lymph nodes or the spleen, where they interact with other cells of the immune system—including B cells, which make antibodies, and killer T cells, which attack microbes and infected cells.
- Cancer vaccines composed of dendritic cells bearing tumor antigens are now in clinical trials involving humans. Scientists are also hoping to turn off the activity of dendritic cells to combat autoimmune diseases such as lupus.

in 1992, when I was at the Schering-Plough Laboratory
for Immunology Research in Dardilly, France, my
co-workers and I devised methods for growing large
amounts of human dendritic cells from bone marrow
stem cells in culture dishes in the laboratory. At roughly
the same time, Steinman—in collaboration with Kayo
Inaba of Kyoto University in Japan and her colleagues—
reported that he had invented a technique for culturing
dendritic cells from mice.

In 1994 researchers led by Antonio Lanzavecchia,
now at the Institute for Research in Biomedicine in
Bellinzona, Switzerland, and Gerold Schuler, now at
the University of Erlangen-Nuremberg in Germany,
found a way to grow the cells from white blood cells
called monocytes. Scientists now know that monocytes
can be prompted to become either dendritic cells, which
turn the immune system on and off, or macrophages,
cells that crawl through the body scavenging dead cells
and microbes.

The ability to culture dendritic cells offered scientists
the opportunity to investigate them in depth for the
first time. Some of the initial discoveries expanded the
tenuous understanding of how dendritic cells function.

There are several subsets of dendritic cells, which
arise from precursors that circulate in the blood and
then take up residence in immature form in the skin,
mucous membranes, and organs such as the lungs and
spleen. Immature dendritic cells are endowed with a
wealth of mechanisms for capturing invading microbes:
they reel in invaders using suction cup–like receptors

on their surfaces, they take microscopic sips of the fluid surrounding them, and they suck in viruses or bacteria by engulfing them in sacks known as vacuoles. Yong-Jun Liu, a former colleague of mine from Schering-Plough who is now at DNAX Research Institute in Palo Alto, Calif., has found that some immature dendritic cells can also zap viruses immediately by secreting a substance called interferon-alpha.

Once they devour foreign objects, the immature cells chop them into fragments (antigens) that can be recognized by the rest of the immune system. The cells use pitchfork-shaped molecules termed the major histocompatibility complex (MHC) to display the antigens on their surfaces. The antigens fit between the tines of the MHC, which comes in two types, class I and class II. The two types vary in shape and in how they acquire their antigen cargo while inside cells.

Dendritic cells are very efficient at capturing and presenting antigens: they can pick up antigens that occur in only minute concentrations. As they process antigens for presentation, they travel to the spleen through the blood or to lymph nodes through a clear fluid known as lymph. Once at their destinations, the cells complete their maturation and present their antigen-laden MHC molecules to naive helper T cells, those that have never encountered antigens before. Dendritic cells are the only cells that can educate naive helper T cells to recognize an antigen as foreign or dangerous. This unique ability appears to derive from co-stimulatory molecules on their surfaces that can bind to corresponding receptors on the T cells.

Once educated, the helper T cells go on to prompt
so-called B cells to produce antibodies that bind to and
inactivate the antigen. The dendritic cells and helper
cells also activate killer T cells, which can destroy cells
infected by microbes. Some of the cells that have been
educated by dendritic cells become "memory" cells
that remain in the body for years—perhaps decades—
to combat the invader in case it ever returns.

Whether the body responds with antibodies or
killer cells seems to be determined in part by which
subset of dendritic cell conveys the message and which
of two types of immune-stimulating substances, called
cytokines, they prompt the helper T cells to make. In
the case of parasites or some bacterial invaders, type 2
cytokines are best because they arm the immune system
with antibodies; type 1 cytokines are better at mustering
killer cells to attack cells infected by other kinds of
bacteria or by viruses.

If a dendritic cell prompts the wrong type of
cytokine, the body can mount the wrong offense.
Generating the appropriate kind of immune response
can be a matter of life or death: when exposed to the
bacterium that causes leprosy, people who mount a
type 1 response develop a mild, tuberculoid form of
the disease, whereas those who have a type 2 response
can end up with the potentially fatal lepromatous form.

Cancer Killers

ACTIVATING NAIVE helper T cells is the basis of vaccines
for everything from pneumonia to tetanus to influenza.

Scientists are now turning the new knowledge of the role that dendritic cells play in immunity against microbes and their toxins into a strategy to fight cancer.

Cancer cells are abnormal and as such are thought to generate molecules that healthy cells don't. If researchers could devise drugs or vaccines that exclusively targeted those aberrant molecules, they could combat cancer more effectively while leaving normal cells and tissues alone—thereby eliminating some of the pernicious side effects of chemotherapy and radiation, such as hair loss, nausea and weakening of the immune system caused by destruction of the bone marrow.

Antigens that occur only on cancerous cells have been hard to find, but researchers have succeeded in isolating several of them, most notably from the skin cancer melanoma. In the early 1990s Thierry Boon of the Ludwig Cancer Institute in Brussels, Steven A. Rosenberg of the National Cancer Institute and their colleagues independently identified melanoma-specific antigens that are currently being targeted in a variety of clinical trials involving humans.

Such trials generally employ vaccines made of dendritic cell precursors that have been isolated from cancer patients and grown in the laboratory together with tumor antigens. During this process, the dendritic cells pick up the antigens, chop them up and present them on their surfaces. When injected back into the patients, the antigen-loaded dendritic cells are expected to ramp up patients' immune response against their own tumors.

Various researchers—including Frank O. Nestle of the University of Zurich and Ronald Levy and Edgar G. Engleman of Stanford University, as well as scientists at several biotechnology companies [*see box on page 48*]—are testing this approach against cancers as diverse as melanoma, B cell lymphoma, and tumors of the prostate and colon. There have been glimmers of success. In September 2001, for instance, my co-workers and I, in collaboration with Steinman's group, reported that 16 of 18 patients with advanced melanoma to whom we gave injections of dendritic cells loaded with melanoma antigens showed signs in laboratory tests of an enhanced immune response to their cancer. What is more, tumor growth was slowed in the nine patients who mounted responses against more than two of the antigens.

Scientists are now working to refine the approach and test it on larger numbers of patients. So far cancer vaccines based on dendritic cells have been tested only in patients with advanced cancer. Although researchers believe that patients with earlier-stage cancers may respond better to the therapy—their immune systems have not yet tried and failed to eradicate their tumor—several potential problems must first be considered.

Some researchers fear that such vaccines might induce patients' immune systems to attack healthy tissue by mistake. For instance, vitiligo—white patches on the skin caused by the destruction of normal pigment-producing melanocytes—has been observed in melanoma patients who have received the earliest antimelanoma vaccines. Conversely, the tumors might mutate to

Dendritic Cell Cancer Vaccines under Development

COMPANY NAME	HEADQUARTERS	STOCK SYMBOL	CANCER TYPE	STATUS*
ML Laboratories	Warrington, England	LSE: MLB	Melanoma	Entering phase I tests
Dendreon	Seattle	Nasdaq: DNDN	Prostate, breast, ovary, colon, multiple myeloma	Phase III (prostate), phase II (prostate, multiple myeloma), phase I (breast, ovary, colon)
Genzyme	Framingham, Mass.	Nasdaq: GZMO	Kidney, melanoma	Phase I (kidney), phase I / II (melanoma)
Immuno-Designed Molecules	Paris	Privately held	Prostate, melanoma	Phase II tests
Merix Bioscience	Durham, N.C.	Privately held	Melanoma	Entering phase I
Oxford BioMedica	Oxford, England	LSE: OXB	Colorectal	Phase I / II
Zycos	Lexington, Mass.	Privately held	DNA-based vaccine against various cancers	Phases I and II

Phase I tests evaluate safety in a small number of patients; phases II and III assess ability to stimulate the immune system and effectiveness in larger numbers of patients.

"escape" the immune onslaught engendered by a dendritic cell vaccine. Tumor cells could accomplish this evasion by no longer making the antigens the vaccine was designed to stimulate the immune system against. This problem is not unique to dendritic cells, though: the same phenomenon can occur with traditional cancer therapies.

In addition, tailoring a dendritic cell vaccine to fight a particular patient's tumors might not be economically feasible. But many scientists are working to circumvent the costly and time-consuming steps of isolating cells from patients and manipulating them in the laboratory for reinjection.

One approach involves prompting dendritic cell precursors already present in a person's body to divide and start orchestrating an immune response against their tumors. David H. Lynch of Immunex in Seattle (recently acquired by Amgen in Thousand Oaks, Calif.) and his co-workers have discovered a cytokine that causes mice to make more dendritic cells, which eventually induce the animals to reject grafted tumors. Other scientists, including Drew M. Pardoll of Johns Hopkins University, have observed that tumor cells that have been genetically engineered to secrete large amounts of cytokines that activate dendritic cells have the most potential as cancer vaccines.

Shutting Immunity Down

IN THE MEANTIME, other scientists are looking at ways to turn off the activity of dendritic cells in instances where they exacerbate disease instead of fighting it. Usually, in a phenomenon known as central tolerance, an organ in the chest called the thymus gets rid of young T cells that happen to recognize the body's own components as foreign before they have a chance to circulate. Some inevitably slip through, however, so the body has a backup mechanism for restraining their activity.

But this mechanism, termed peripheral tolerance, appears to be broken in patients with autoimmune disorders such as rheumatoid arthritis, type 1 diabetes and systemic lupus erythematosus. Last year my colleagues and I reported that dendritic cells from the blood of people with lupus are unnaturally active. Cells from these patients release high amounts of interferon-alpha, an immune-stimulating protein that causes precursors to grow into mature dendritic cells while still in the bloodstream. The mature cells then ingest DNA, which is present in unusual amounts in the blood of people with lupus, and that in turn causes the individual's immune system to generate antibodies against his or her own DNA. These antibodies result in the life-threatening complications of lupus when they lodge in the kidneys or the walls of blood vessels. Accordingly, we propose that blocking interferon-alpha might lead to a therapy for lupus by preventing dendritic cell activation. A similar strategy might prevent organ transplant recipients from rejecting their new tissues.

A new treatment for AIDS might also rest on a better understanding of dendritic cells. In 2000 Carl G. Figdor and Yvette van Kooyk of the University Medical Center St. Radboud in Nijmegen, the Netherlands, identified a subset of dendritic cells that makes DC-SIGN, a molecule that can bind to the outer coat of HIV. These cells pick up HIV as they regularly prowl the mucous membranes and deep tissues. When they travel to the lymph nodes, they unwittingly deliver the virus to a large concentration of T cells. Drugs that block the interaction between DC-SIGN and HIV might slow the progression of AIDS.

Other infectious diseases—including malaria, measles and cytomegalovirus—also manipulate dendritic cells for their own ends. Red blood cells that have been infected by malaria parasites, for instance, bind to dendritic cells and prevent them from maturing and alerting the immune system to the presence of the invaders. Several groups of researchers are now devising approaches to prevent such microbes from hijacking dendritic cells; some are even seeking to use super-charged dendritic cells to fight the infections.

As we learn more about the molecules that control dendritic cells, we will find ways to harness their therapeutic potential. The increasing number of scientists and corporations working on dendritic cells portends that we will soon be able to maximize the biological power of these cells to treat and prevent the diseases that plague humankind.

The Author

JACQUES BANCHEREAU has directed the Baylor Institute for Immunology Research in Dallas since 1996. The institute aims to manipulate the human immune system to treat cancer as well as infectious and autoimmune diseases. Before 1996 Banchereau led the Schering-Plough Laboratory for Immunology Research in Dardilly, France. He obtained his Ph.D. in biochemistry from the University of Paris. Banchereau holds many patents on immunological techniques and is a member of the scientific advisory board of Merix Bioscience, a biotechnology company based in Durham, N.C.

More to Explore

"Dendritic Cells and the Control of Immunity." Jacques Banchereau and Ralph M. Steinman in *Nature*, Vol. 392, pages 245–252; March 19, 1998.

"Dendritic Cells as Vectors for Therapy." Jacques Banchereau, Beatrice Schuler-Thurner, A. Karolina Palucka and Gerold Schuler in *Cell*, Vol. 106, No. 3, pages 271–274; August 10, 2001.

Background information on the immune system and on experimental cancer therapies such as those using dendritic cells can be found on the American Cancer Society's Web site: **www.cancer.org**

"New Light on
4. Medicine"

by Nick Lane

*Pigments that turn caustic on exposure to light can fight cancer,
blindness and heart disease. Their light-induced toxicity may
also help explain the origin of vampire tales*

Stories of vampires date back thousands of years.
Our modern concept stems from Bram Stoker's
quirky classic *Dracula* and Hollywood's Bela Lugosi—
the romantic, sexually charged, blood-sucking
outcast with a fatal susceptibility to sunlight and an
abhorrence of garlic and crosses. In contrast, vampires
of folklore cut a pathetic figure and were also known
as the undead. In searching for some underlying
truth in vampire stories, researchers have speculated
that the tales may have been inspired by real people
who suffered from a rare blood disease, porphyria.
And in seeking treatments for this disorder, scientists
have stumbled on a new way to attack other, more
common serious ills.

Porphyria is actually a collection of related diseases
in which pigments called porphyrins accumulate in
the skin, bones and teeth. Many porphyrins are
benign in the dark but are transformed by sunlight
into caustic, flesh-eating toxins. Without treatment,
the worst forms of the disease (such as congenital
erythropoietic porphyria) can be grotesque, ultimately
exacting the kind of hideous disfigurement one might

expect of the undead. The victims' ears and nose get eaten away. Their lips and gums erode to reveal red, fanglike teeth. Their skin acquires a patchwork of scars, dense pigmentation and deathly pale hues, reflecting underlying anemia. Because anemia can be treated with blood transfusions, some historians speculate that in the dark ages people with porphyria might have tried drinking blood as a folk remedy. Whatever the truth of this claim, those with congenital erythropoietic porphyria would certainly have learned not to venture outside during the day. They might have learned to avoid garlic, too, for some chemicals in garlic are thought to exacerbate the symptoms of the disease porphyria, turning a mild attack into an agonizing reaction.

While struggling to find a cure for porphyria, scientists came to realize that porphyrins could be not just a problem but a tool for medicine. If a porphyrin is injected into diseased tissue, such as a cancerous tumor, it can be activated by light to destroy that tissue. The procedure is known as photodynamic therapy, or PDT, and has grown from an improbable treatment for cancer in the 1970s to a sophisticated and effective weapon against a diverse array of malignancies today and, most recently, for macular degeneration and pathologic myopia, common causes of adult blindness. Ongoing research includes pioneering treatments for coronary artery disease, AIDS, autoimmune diseases, transplantation rejection and leukemia.

Molecular Mechanisms

THE SUBSTANCES AT THE HEART of porphyria and photo-dynamic therapy are among the oldest and most important of all biological molecules, because they orchestrate the two most critical energy-generating processes of life: photosynthesis and oxygen respiration. Porphyrins make up a large family of closely related compounds, a colorful set of evolutionary variations on a theme. All porphyrins have in common a flat ring (composed of carbon and nitrogen) with a central hole, which provides space for a metal ion such as iron or magnesium to bind to it. When aligned correctly in the grip of the porphyrin rings, these metal atoms catalyze the most fundamental energy-generating processes in biology. Chlorophyll, the plant pigment that absorbs the energy of sunlight in photosynthesis, is a porphyrin, as is heme, which is at the heart of the oxygen-transporter protein hemoglobin and of many enzymes vital for life, including cytochrome oxidase (which generates energy by transferring electrons to oxygen in a critical step of cellular respiration).

Porphyria arises because of a flaw in the body's heme-making machinery. The body produces heme and other porphyrins in a series of eight coordinated stages, each catalyzed by a separate enzyme. Iron is added at the end to make heme. In porphyria, one of the steps does not occur, leading to a backlog of the intermediate compounds produced earlier in the sequence. The body has not evolved to dispose of these intermediates efficiently, so it dumps them, often in the skin. The intermediates do not damage the skin directly, but many of them cause trouble indirectly. Metal-free porphyrins (as well as metalloporphyrins containing metals that do not interact with the porphyrin ring) can become excited when they absorb light at certain wavelengths; their electrons jump into higher-energy orbitals. The molecules can then transmit their excitation to other molecules having the right kind of bonds, especially oxygen, to produce reactive singlet oxygen and other highly reactive and destructive molecules known as free radicals. Metal-free porphyrins, in other words, are not the agents, but rather the brokers, of destruction. They catalyze the production of toxic forms of oxygen.

Photosensitive reactions are not necessarily harmful. Their beneficial effects have been known since ancient times. In particular, some seeds and fruits contain photosensitive chemicals (photosensitizers) called psoralens, which indirectly led scientists to experiment

Overview/Light Therapy

- In photodynamic therapy, light-activated chemicals called porphyrins are used to destroy fast-growing cells and tissue. Doctors could apply the treatment to a variety of ailments, including age-related macular degeneration, tumors and atherosclerotic plaques.
- A few porphyrin drugs are on the market, and several others are undergoing human trials.
- Researchers got the idea for photodynamic therapy from their knowledge of the rare disease porphyria, in which porphyrins accumulate in the skin and certain organs. Unless the disease is managed, victims of the severest type of porphyria can become disfigured, leading some researchers to speculate that they may have inspired medieval vampire legends.

with porphyrins. Psoralens have been used to treat skin conditions in Egypt and India for several thousand years. They were first incorporated into modern medicine by Egyptian dermatologist Abdel Monem El Mofty of Cairo University, just over 50 years ago, when he began treating patients with vitiligo (a disease that leaves irregular patches of skin without pigment) and, later, those with psoriasis using purified psoralens and sunlight. When activated by light, psoralens react with DNA in proliferating cells to kill them.

Two American dermatologists, Aaron B. Lerner of Yale University and Thomas B. Fitzpatrick of Harvard University, were struck by the potential of psoralens. In the 1960s they showed that psoralens are activated by ultraviolet (UVA) rays, and the researchers later refined psoralen therapy using an ultraviolet lamp similar to those used in solariums today. Their method became known as PUVA (short for psoralen with UVA) and is now one of the most effective treatments for psoriasis and other skin conditions.

A Way to Kill Cancer Cells?

IN THE EARLY 1970s the success of PUVA impressed Thomas J. Dougherty of the Roswell Park Cancer Institute in Buffalo, N.Y., leading him to wonder if a variant of it could be effective against cancer. Activated psoralens can kill rogue cells to settle inflammation, but in comparison with porphyrins they are not potent photosensitizers. If psoralens could kill individual cells,

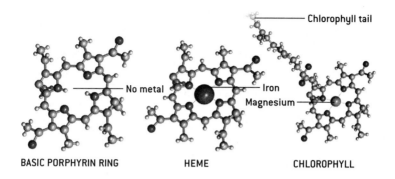

Chlorophyll tail

No metal
Iron
Magnesium

BASIC PORPHYRIN RING   HEME   CHLOROPHYLL

PORPHYRINS all have in common a flat ring, mainly composed of carbon and nitrogen, and a central hole where a metal ion can sit. The basic ring (*far left*) becomes caustic when exposed to light; molecules useful for photo-dynamic therapy also share this trait. Nontoxic examples include heme (a component of the oxygen transporter hemoglobin) and the chlorophyll that converts light to energy in plants.

could porphyrins perhaps devour whole tumors? His idea was the beginning of true photodynamic therapy, in which photosensitizers catalyze the production of oxygen free radicals. It was built on earlier work, which revealed two medically useful properties of the porphyrins: they accumulate selectively in cancer cells and are activated by red light, which penetrates more deeply into biological tissues than do shorter wavelengths, such as blue light or UVA.

Dougherty injected a mixture of porphyrins into the bloodstream of mice with mammary tumors. He then waited a couple days for the porphyrins to build up in the tumors before shining red light on them. His early setup was primitive and passed the light from an old slide projector through a 35mm slide colored red.

His results were nonetheless spectacular. The light activated the porphyrins within the tumor, which transferred their energy to oxygen in cells to damage the surrounding tissues. In almost every case, the tumors blackened and died after the light treatment. There were no signs of recurrence.

Dougherty and his colleagues published their data in 1975 in the *Journal of the National Cancer Institute*, with the brave title "Photoradiation Therapy II: Cure of Animal Tumors with Hematoporphyrin and Light." Over the next few years they refined their technique by using a low-power laser to focus red light onto the tumors. They went on to treat more than 100 patients in this way, including people with cancers of the breast, lung, prostate and skin. Their outcomes were gratifying, with a "complete or partial response" in 111 of 113 tumors.

Sadly, though, cancer is not so easily beaten. As more physicians started trying their hand with PDT, some serious drawbacks began to emerge. The affinity of porphyrins for tumors turned out to be a bit of an illusion—porphyrins are taken up by any rapidly proliferating tissue, including the skin, leading to photosensitivity. Although Dougherty's original patients were no doubt careful to avoid the sun, nearly 40 percent of them reported burns and skin rashes in the weeks after PDT.

Potency was another issue. The early porphyrin preparations were mixtures, and they were seldom strong enough to kill the entire tumor. Some porphyrins are not efficient at passing energy to oxygen; others are activated only by light that cannot penetrate more than a few millimeters into the tumor. Some biological pigments normally present in tissues, such as hemoglobin and melanin, also absorb light and in doing so can prevent a porphyrin from being activated. Even the porphyrin itself can cause this problem if it accumulates to such high levels that it absorbs all the light in the superficial layers of the tumor, thus preventing penetration into the deeper layers.

Many of these difficulties could not be resolved without the help of specialists from other disciplines. Chemists were needed to create new, synthetic porphyrins, ones that had greater selectivity for tumors and greater potency and that would be activated by wavelengths of light able to reach farther into tissues and tumors. (For each porphyrin, light activation and absorption occur only at particular wavelengths, so the trick is to design a porphyrin that has its absorption maximum at a wavelength that penetrates into biological tissues.) Physicists were needed to design sources that could produce light of particular wavelengths to activate the new porphyrins or that could be attached to fine endoscopes and catheters or even implanted in tissues. Pharmacologists were needed to devise ways of reducing the time that porphyrins spent circulating in the bloodstream, thereby restricting photosensitive side effects. Finally, clinicians were needed to design trials that could prove an effect and determine the best treatment regimens.

The ideal drug would be not only potent and highly selective for tumors but also broken down quickly into harmless compounds and excreted from the body. The first commercial preparation, porfimer sodium (Photofrin), was approved by the U.S. Food and Drug Administration for the treatment of various cancers. Although it has been helpful against certain cancers (including esophageal, bladder, head and neck, and skin cancers and some stages of lung cancer), it has not been the breakthrough that had been hoped for and cannot yet be considered an integral part of cancer therapy. Surprisingly, though, the first photosensitizing drug to fulfill most of the stringent criteria for potency and efficacy without causing photosensitivity, verteporfin (Visudyne), was approved in April 2000 by the FDA not to treat cancer at all but to prevent blindness. As the theories converged with reality, researchers came to realize that PDT can do far more than destroy tumors.

Battling Blindness

ONE THING IT COULD DO, for instance, was combat age-related macular degeneration (AMD), the most common cause of legal blindness in our maturing Western population [see "The Challenge of Macular Degeneration," by Hui Sun and Jeremy Nathans; SCIENTIFIC AMERICAN, October 2001]. Most people who acquire AMD have a benign form and do not lose their sight, but about a tenth have a much more aggressive type called wet AMD. In this case, abnormal, leaking blood vessels, like miniature knots of varicose veins, grow underneath the retina and ultimately damage the sharp central vision required for reading and driving. As the disease progresses, central vision is obliterated, making it impossible to recognize people's faces or the details of objects.

Most attempts to hinder this grimly inexorable process have failed. Dietary antioxidants may be able to delay the onset of the disorder but have little effect on the progression of established disease. Until recently, the only treatment proved to slow the progression of wet AMD was a technique called laser photocoagulation. The procedure involves applying a thermal laser to the blood vessels to fuse them and thus halt their growth. Unfortunately, the laser also burns the normal retina and so destroys a small region to prevent later loss of vision in the rest of the eye. Whether this is worth it depends on the area of the retina that needs to be treated. For most people diagnosed with wet AMD, the area is located below the critical central part of vision or is already too large to benefit from laser coagulation.

Against this depressing backdrop, researchers at Harvard and at the biotechnology firm QLT, Inc., in Vancouver, B.C., reasoned that PDT might halt the growth of these blood vessels and delay or even prevent blindness. If porphyrins could accumulate in any rapidly proliferating tissue—the very problem in cancer—then perhaps they could also accumulate in the blood vessels growing under the retina. Verteporfin, a novel synthetic porphyrin, seemed promising because it had a good track record in preclinical, animal studies at QLT and at the University of British Columbia in the late 1980s and early 1990s.

Verteporfin accumulates in abnormal retinal vessels remarkably quickly: within 15 minutes of injection into an arm vein. When activated by red laser light, verteporfin seals off the vessels, sparing the overlying retina. Any blood vessels that grow back can be nipped in the bud by further treatments. Two major clinical trials, headed by Neil M. Bressler of the Wilmer Eye Institute at Johns Hopkins University, confirmed that PDT can be given six or seven times over a three-year period without damaging a healthy retina. For people with the most aggressive form of AMD (with mostly "classic" lesions), verteporfin halved the risk of moderate or serious vision loss over a two-year period. The effect is sustained over at least three or four years: patients who are not treated lose as much vision in three months as those treated with verteporfin lose in three years. The treatment also worked, though not as well, for people with less aggressive types of AMD and for those with related diseases such as pathologic myopia and ocular histoplasmosis syndrome. Only a small proportion of patients suffered from sunburns or other adverse reactions, rarely more than 24 hours after the procedure was done.

Some participants in the trials gained little benefit from PDT. For many of them, the disease may have already progressed too far. A reanalysis of clinical data presented by Bressler in April 2002 at the International Congress of Ophthalmology in Sydney, Australia, showed that smaller lesions respond much better to treatment than older, larger ones, implying that early detection and treatment may optimize the benefits of PDT.

How Photodynamic Therapy Works

DOCTORS WHO ADMINISTER photodynamic therapy deliver photosensitive chemicals called porphyrins intravenously. These chemicals then collect in rapidly proliferating cells and, when exposed to light, initiate a cascade of molecular reactions that can destroy those cells and the tissues they compose. Some targets for the therapy include abnormal blood vessels in the retinas of people with age-related macular degeneration (the leading cause of adult blindness), cancerous tumors and atherosclerotic plaques in coronary arteries.

. . . AT THE MOLECULAR LEVEL

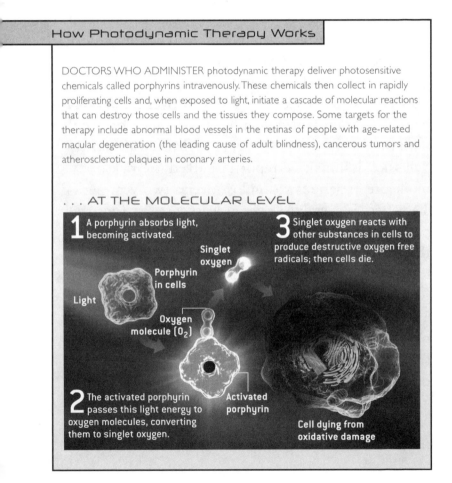

1 A porphyrin absorbs light, becoming activated.

Singlet oxygen

Porphyrin in cells

Light

Oxygen molecule (O_2)

2 The activated porphyrin passes this light energy to oxygen molecules, converting them to singlet oxygen.

Activated porphyrin

3 Singlet oxygen reacts with other substances in cells to produce destructive oxygen free radicals; then cells die.

Cell dying from oxidative damage

. . . IN THE EYE

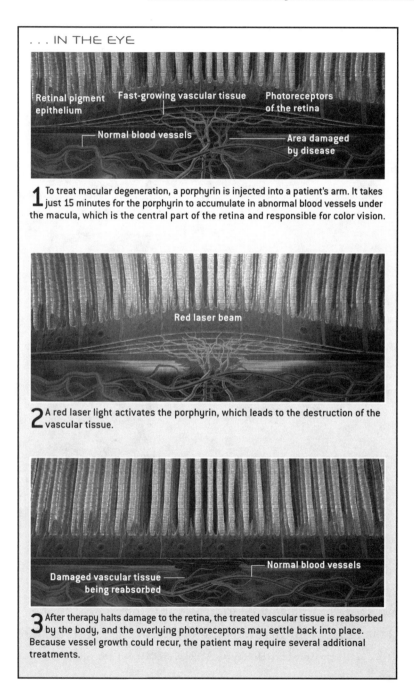

Retinal pigment epithelium | Fast-growing vascular tissue | Photoreceptors of the retina

Normal blood vessels | Area damaged by disease

1 To treat macular degeneration, a porphyrin is injected into a patient's arm. It takes just 15 minutes for the porphyrin to accumulate in abnormal blood vessels under the macula, which is the central part of the retina and responsible for color vision.

Red laser beam

2 A red laser light activates the porphyrin, which leads to the destruction of the vascular tissue.

Normal blood vessels

Damaged vascular tissue being reabsorbed

3 After therapy halts damage to the retina, the treated vascular tissue is reabsorbed by the body, and the overlying photoreceptors may settle back into place. Because vessel growth could recur, the patient may require several additional treatments.

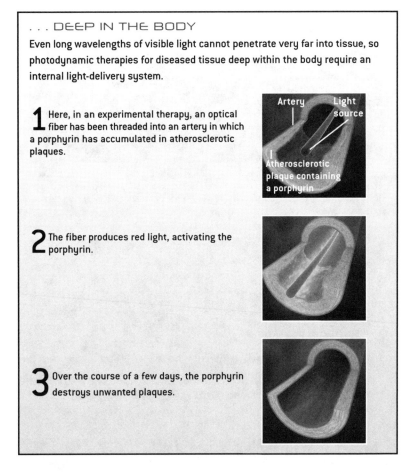

... DEEP IN THE BODY

Even long wavelengths of visible light cannot penetrate very far into tissue, so photodynamic therapies for diseased tissue deep within the body require an internal light-delivery system.

1 Here, in an experimental therapy, an optical fiber has been threaded into an artery in which a porphyrin has accumulated in atherosclerotic plaques.

Artery   Light source

Atherosclerotic plaque containing a porphyrin

2 The fiber produces red light, activating the porphyrin.

3 Over the course of a few days, the porphyrin destroys unwanted plaques.

Other Treatment Avenues

THE SUCCESS OF OPHTHALMIC PDT has inspired research activity in other fields but also reveals the drawbacks of the treatment. In particular, even red light penetrates no more than a few centimeters into biological tissues. This limitation threatens the utility of PDT in internal medicine—its significance might seem to be skin deep.

There are ways of turning PDT inward, however. One ingenious idea is called photoangioplasty, which is now being used to treat coronary artery disease.

Coronary angioplasty is a minimally invasive procedure for treating arteries affected by atherosclerosis. It uses a tiny balloon to open arteries, so that atherosclerotic plaques do not occlude the entire vessel. Photoangioplasty could sidestep many of the problems of conventional angioplasty, notably the restenosis (renarrowing) of treated arteries. The procedure involves injecting a porphyrin into the bloodstream, waiting for it to build up in the damaged arterial walls and then illuminating the artery from the inside, using a tiny light source attached to the end of a catheter. The light activates the porphyrins in the plaques, destroying the abnormal tissues while sparing the normal walls of the artery. The results of a small human trial testing the safety of the synthetic porphyrin motexafin lutetium were presented in March 2002 by Jeffrey J. Popma of Brigham and Women's Hospital at the annual meeting of the American College of Cardiology. Although it is still early in the testing process, the findings fuel hopes for the future: the procedure was safe, and its success at preventing restenosis increased as the dosage increased.

Accumulation of porphyrins in active and proliferating cells raises the possibility of treating other conditions in which abnormal cell activation or proliferation plays a role—among them, infectious diseases. Attempts to treat infections with the pigments had long

Photodynamic Therapies

THE LIGHT-ACTIVATED drugs listed below are a sampling of those on the market or in development.

DRUG	TARGET	MAKER	STATUS
Levulan (5-aminolevulinic acid)	Acne and actinic keratosis (a pre-cancerous skin disorder), Barrett's esophagus), (a pre-cancerous condition)	DUSA PHARMA-CEUTICALS Toronto	On the market for actinic keratosis; Phase II trials (relatively small studies in humans) have been completed for Barrett's esophagus
Photofrin (porfimer sodium)	Cancers of the esophagus and lung, high-grade dysplasia from Barrett's esophagus	AXCAN SCANDIPHARM Birmingham, Ala.	On the market for esophageal cancer and nonsmall cell lung cancer; awaiting FDA decision on high-grade dysplasia
Visudyne (verteporfin)	Age-related macular degeneration, pathologic myopia and ocular histoplasmosis (eye disorders)	QLT, INC., and NOVARTIS OPHTHALMICS Vancouver, B.C., and Duluth, Ga.	On the market
Metvix (methyl-aminolevulinic acid)	Actinic keratosis, basal cell skin cancer and squamous cell skin cancer	PHOTOCURE Oslo, Norway	Awaiting final FDA approval for actinic keratosis; in Phase III trials (large studies of efficacy) for skin cancers
PhotoPoint SnET2 (tin ethyl etiopurpurin)	Age-related macular degeneration	MIRAVANT MEDICAL TECHNOLOGIES Santa Barbara, Calif.	Phase III trials have been completed
verteporfin	Basal cell cancer, androgenetic alopecia (male pattern baldness) and prostatic hyperplasia (enlarged prostate)	QLT, INC.	In Phase III trials for basal cell cancer; as QLT0074, in Phase I trials (tests of safety in small numbers of patients) for other conditions

DRUG	TARGET	MAKER	STATUS
PhotoPoint MV9411 (contains indium)	Plaque psoriasis	MIRAVANT MEDICAL TECHNOLOGIES	In Phase II trials
Antrin (motexafin lutetium)	Diseased arteries	PHARMACYCLICS Sunnyvale, Calif.	Phase II trials for peripheral artery disease and Phase I trials for coronary artery disease have been completed
Lutrin (motexafin lutetium)	Cancerous tumors	PHARMACYCLICS	In Phase I trials for prostate cancer and cervical intraepithelial neoplasia

been frustrated by a limited effect on gram-negative bacteria, which have a complex cell wall that obstructs the uptake of porphyrins into these organisms. One solution, developed by Michael R. Hamblin and his colleagues at Harvard, involved attaching a polymer—usually polylysine, a repetitive chain of the amino acid lysine—to the porphyrin. The polymer disrupts the lipid structure of the bacterial cell wall, enabling the porphyrins to gain entry to the cell. Once inside, they can be activated by light to kill the bacteria. In recent studies of animals with oral infections and infected wounds, the altered porphyrin showed potent antimicrobial activity against a broad spectrum of gram-negative and gram-positive bacteria. As antibiotic resistance becomes more intractable, targeted antimicrobial PDT could become a useful weapon in the medical arsenal.

Several other, related photodynamic methods hinge on the finding that activated immune cells take up greater amounts of photosensitizing drugs than do quiescent immune cells and red blood cells, sparing the quiet cells from irreversible damage. In most infections, nobody would wish to destroy activated immune cells: they are, after all, responsible for the body's riposte to the infection. In these cases, targeting immune cells would be equivalent to "friendly fire" and would give the infection free rein to pillage the body.

In AIDS, however, the reverse is true. The AIDS virus, HIV, infects the immune cells themselves. Targeting infected immune cells would then be more like eliminating double agents. In the laboratory, HIV-infected immune cells take up porphyrins, thereby becoming vulnerable to light treatment. In patients, the light could be applied either by withdrawing blood, illuminating it and transfusing it back into the body (extracorporeal phototherapy) or by shining red light onto the skin, in what is called transdermal phototherapy. In the transdermal approach, light would eliminate activated immune cells in the circulation as they passed through the skin. Whether the technique will be potent enough to eliminate diseased immune cells in HIV-infected patients remains an open question.

Autoimmune diseases, rejection of organ transplants, and leukemias are also all linked by the common thread of activated and proliferating immune cells. In autoimmune diseases, components of our own body erroneously activate immune cells. These activated clones then proliferate in an effort to destroy the perceived threat—say, the myelin sheath in multiple sclerosis or the collagen in rheumatoid arthritis. When organs are implanted, activated immune cells may multiply to reject the foreign tissue—the transplanted organ or even the body tissues of the new host, in the case of bone marrow transplants. In leukemia, immune cells and their precursors in the bone marrow produce large numbers of nonfunctional cells. In each instance, PDT could potentially eliminate the unwanted immune cells, while preserving the quiescent cells, to maintain a normal immune response to infection. As in HIV infection, the procedure might work either extracorporeally or transdermally. Much of this research is in late-stage preclinical or early clinical trials. For all the cleverness in exploring possible medical applications, though, we can only hope that more extensive clinical studies will bear fruit.

The Author

NICK LANE studied biochemistry at Imperial College, University of London. His doctoral research, at the Royal Free Hospital, concentrated on oxygen free radicals and metabolic function in organ transplants. Lane is an honorary senior research fellow at University College London and strategic director at Adelphi Medi Cine, a medical multimedia company based in London. His book, *Oxygen: The Molecule That Made the World*, was published in the U.S. by Oxford University Press in the spring of 2003.

More to Explore

The Colours of Life: An Introduction to the Chemistry
of Porphyrins and Related Compounds. L. R.
Milgrom. Oxford University Press, 1997.
"Lethal Weapon." P. Moore in *New Scientist*, Vol. 158,
No. 2130, pages 40–43; April 18, 1998.
"Verteporfin Therapy for Subfoveal Choroidal
Neovascularization in Age-Related Macular
Degeneration: Three-Year Results of an Open-
Label Extension of 2 Randomized Clinical Trials."
TAP Report No. 5. M. S. Blumenkranz et al. in
Archives of Ophthalmology, Vol. 120, No. 10,
pages 1307–1317; October 2002.
Oxygen: The Molecule That Made the World. Nick
Lane. Oxford University Pressm, April 2003.
An overview of the nature of and treatments for
porphyria can be found at **www.sciam.com/
explore_directory.cfm**

5. "Tumor-Busting Viruses"

by Dirk M. Nettelbeck and David T. Curiel

*A new technique called virotherapy harnesses viruses,
those banes of humankind, to stop another scourge—cancer*

Viruses are some of the most insidious creations in nature. They travel light: equipped with just their genetic material packed tightly inside a crystalline case of protein, they latch onto cells, insert their genes, and co-opt the cells' gene-copying and protein-making machinery, using them to make billions of copies of themselves. Once formed, the new viruses percolate to the cell surface, pinch off inside minuscule bubbles of cell membrane and drift away, or else they continue reproducing until the cell finally bursts. In any case, they go on to infect and destroy other cells, resulting in diseases from AIDS to the common cold.

Different viruses cause different diseases in part because each virus enters a cell by first attaching to a specific suction-cuplike receptor on its surface. Liver cells display one kind of receptor used by one family of viruses, whereas nerve cells display another receptor used by a different viral family, so each type of virus infects a particular variety of cell. Cancer researchers have envied this selectivity for years: if they could only target cancer therapies to tumor cells and avoid damaging normal ones, they might be able

ADENOVIRUSES explode from a cancer cell that has been selectively infected in order to kill it. The viruses can spread to and wipe out other tumor cells.

to eliminate many of the noxious side effects of cancer treatment.

Some scientists, including ourselves, are now genetically engineering a range of viruses that act as search-and-destroy missiles: selectively infecting and killing cancer cells while leaving healthy ones alone. This new strategy, called virotherapy, has shown promise in animal tests, and clinical trials involving human patients are now under way. Researchers are evaluating virotherapy alone and as a novel means for administering traditional chemotherapies solely to tumor cells. They are also developing methods to label viruses with radioactive or fluorescent tags in order to track the movement of the viral agents in patients.

Viruses to the Rescue?

ONE OF THE FIRST INKLINGS that viruses could be useful in combating cancer came in 1912, when an Italian gynecologist observed the regression of cervical cancer in a woman who was inoculated with a rabies vaccine made from a live, crippled form of the rabies virus. Physicians first injected viruses into cancer patients intentionally in the late 1940s, but only a handful appeared to benefit. Twenty years later scientists found that a virus that causes the veterinary disorder Newcastle disease shows a preference for infecting tumor cells and began to try to enhance that tendency by growing the viruses for generations in human cancer cells in laboratory culture dishes. Although critics countered that such viruses could be exerting only an indirect effect against cancer by generally activating an individual's immune system and making it more likely to detect and kill cancer cells, reports continued to pop up in the medical literature linking viral infection and cancer remission. In the early 1970s and 1980s two groups of physicians described patients whose lymphomas shrank after they came down with measles.

The modern concept of virotherapy began in the late 1990s, when researchers led by Frank McCormick of ONYX Pharmaceuticals in Richmond, Calif., and Daniel R. Henderson of Calydon in Sunnyvale, Calif., independently published reports showing they could target virotherapy to human cancer cells grafted into mice, thereby eliminating the human tumors. (ONYX is no longer developing therapeutic viruses, and Calydon has been acquired by Cell Genesys in South San Francisco, Calif.) Both groups used adenovirus, a cause of the common cold that has been intensively explored for virotherapy. (Other viruses under study include herpes simplex, parvovirus, vaccinia and reovirus.) Adenovirus is appealing in part because researchers understand its biology very well after years of trying to cure colds and of using the virus in molecular biology and gene therapy research. It consists of a 20-sided protein case, or capsid, filled with DNA and equipped with 12 protein "arms." These protrusions have evolved over millennia to latch onto a cellular receptor whose normal function is to help cells adhere to one another.

Adenoviruses are distinct from the types of viruses usually used in gene therapy to treat inherited disorders. Gene therapy traditionally employs retroviruses to splice a functioning copy of a gene permanently into the body of a patient in whom that gene has ceased to work

Overview/Anticancer Viruses

- Virotherapy is a new strategy to treat cancer by selectively infecting and killing tumor cells. Researchers are testing various approaches to target viruses—particularly adenoviruses—to cancer cells, leaving normal cells untouched.
- The viruses used in virotherapy can either kill tumor cells by bursting them open or deliver genes that make the cells more susceptible to traditional chemotherapies.
- The same types of viruses used in virotherapy can also be labeled with fluorescent or radioactive tags. Once delivered into the body, they home in on cancer cells. In the future, physicians might be able to use this imaging technique to detect the presence of tiny tumors.

properly. Unlike retroviruses, however, adenoviruses do not integrate their DNA into the genes of cells they infect; the genes they ferry into a cell usually work only for a while and then break down. Scientists have investigated adenoviruses extensively in gene therapy approaches to treat cancer, in which the viruses are armed with genes that, for example, make cancer cells more susceptible than normal ones to chemotherapy. In general, tests involving adenoviruses have been safe, but regrettably a volunteer died in 1999 after receiving an infusion of adenoviruses as part of a clinical trial to test a potential gene therapy for a genetic liver disorder [*see box on page 82*].

Gene therapists have been working to tailor adenoviruses and other viral vectors, or gene-delivery systems, to improve their safety and reduce the chances that such a tragedy might occur again. It is perhaps even more essential for researchers, such as ourselves, who are investigating virotherapy to develop safer, more targeted vectors, because virotherapy by definition aims to kill the cells the viruses infect, not just insert a therapeutic gene into them. Killing the wrong cells could be dangerous.

Adenoviruses bring with them characteristics that can make them riskier or safer, depending on the circumstances. Nearly everyone has been exposed at one time or another to adenoviruses, so almost all of us carry antibodies the immune system makes to target them for destruction. Accordingly, shots of adenoviruses as cancer therapies might cause severe, flulike symptoms if the body recognizes them as foreign and ramps up an immune response to eradicate them. (Wiping out the viruses would also squelch the therapy.) At the same time, recognition by the immune system ensures that the viruses do not reproduce out of control. Investigators are now designing various therapeutic approaches to optimize the efficacy of virotherapy and minimize the chances that adenoviruses will cause side effects. These strategies include giving immunosuppressive drugs at the time of virotherapy and modifying the adenoviruses so that they do not trigger a reaction by the immune system.

Homing In on the Target

VIROTHERAPISTS ARE DEVISING two main strategies to make sure their missiles hit their objectives accurately with no collateral damage. In the first approach, termed transductional targeting, researchers are attempting to adapt the viruses so that they preferentially infect, or transduce, cancer cells. The second method, called transcriptional targeting, involves altering the viruses so that their genes can be active, or transcribed, only in tumors.

Transductional targeting is particularly necessary because, unfortunately, adenoviruses bind more efficiently to the variety of normal tissues in the human body than they do to most tumor cells. We can reverse this pattern using specially generated adapter molecules made of antibodies that snap onto the arms of the virus like sockets on a socket wrench. By attaching carefully chosen antibodies or other molecules that selectively bind only to a specific protein found on tumor cells, we can render adenoviruses unable to infect any cells but cancerous ones. Once the antibody-bearing virus latches onto a targeted cell, the hapless cell engulfs it in a membrane sac and pulls it inside. As the sac disintegrates, the viral capsid travels to a pore in the cell's nucleus and injects its own DNA. Soon the viral DNA directs the cell to make copies of the viral DNA, synthesize viral proteins and combine the two into billions of new adenoviruses. When the cell is full to capacity, the virus activates a "death gene" and prompts the cell to burst, releasing the new viruses to spread to other cells.

The viruses can also be engineered more directly. In this regard, Curiel's group at the University of Alabama's Gene Therapy Center has designed adeno-viruses that bind to cellular proteins called integrins. These molecules help cells stick to the network of connective tissue, called the extracellular matrix, that organizes the cells into cohesive tissues. Although integrins are also made by healthy cells, cancer cells produce them in abundance as they become metastatic and begin to squeeze through tissue layers and travel throughout the body. The University of Alabama research group has had encouraging results using the engineered viruses in mice bearing human ovarian cancers. The viruses homed in on the ovarian tumor cells and killed them, ridding the treated animals of the disease.

Transcriptional targeting generally takes advantage of genetic switches (promoters) that dictate how often a given gene is functional (gives rise to the protein it encodes) in a particular type of cell. Although each body cell contains the same encyclopedia of genetic information, some cells use different chapters of the encyclopedia more often than others in order to fulfill their specialized tasks. Skin cells called melanocytes, for instance, must make much more of the pigment melanin than liver cells, which have little use for the protein. Accordingly, the promoter for the key enzyme for making melanin gets turned on in melanocytes but generally is off in most other body tissues. In the deadly skin cancer melanoma, the gene encoding this enzyme is fully functional, making the tumors appear black. We, and others, have engineered adenoviruses that have a promoter for the enzyme adjacent to genes that are essential for the viruses' ability to replicate. Although these viruses might infect normal cells, such as liver cells, they can reproduce only inside melanocytes, which contain the special combination of proteins needed to turn on the promoter.

Researchers are currently tailoring adenoviruses with a variety of promoters that limit their activity to particular organs or tissues. In liver cancers, for example, the promoter for the gene a-fetoprotein—which is normally shut down after fetal development—becomes reactivated. Adenoviruses containing that same promoter hold promise for eradicating liver tumors. Scientists led by Jonathan W. Simons at Johns Hopkins University have tested the approach in men whose prostate cancer recurred following treatment with radiation. The researchers used adenoviruses that had been engineered by Cell Genesys to contain the promoter for prostate-specific antigen, a protein made in abundance by prostate tumors. They administered the virotherapy to 20 men who received varying doses of the adenoviruses. In 2001 Simons and his colleagues reported that none of the men experienced serious side effects and that the tumors of the five men who received the highest doses of the virotherapy shrank by at least 50 percent.

Other Strategies

VIROTHERAPISTS MIGHT END UP combining the transductional and transcriptional targeting strategies to ensure that the viruses kill only tumor cells and not normal ones. Adenoviruses engineered to contain the promoter for the enzyme that makes melanin, for instance, can also replicate in normal melanocytes, so on their own they might cause spots of depigmentation. And adenoviruses that are designed to bind to receptors on the surfaces of tumor cells can still invade a small proportion of healthy cells. But viruses altered to have several fail-safe mechanisms would be expected to be less likely to harm normal cells. There are no results at present, however, to demonstrate that a combination of approaches makes viruses more targeted.

A further strategy for targeting virotherapy makes the most of one of cancer's hallmarks: the ability of tumor cells to divide again and again in an uncontrolled manner. Healthy cells make proteins that serve as natural brakes on cell division—notably, the retinoblastoma (Rb) and p53 proteins. As cells turn cancerous, however, the

But Is It Safe?

Many approaches to virotherapy use adenoviruses, which caused a death in a clinical trial of gene therapy four years ago

In September 1999 18-year-old Jesse Gelsinger died after receiving an infusion of adenoviruses into his liver. He had a mild form of an inherited liver disease called ornithine transcarbamylase deficiency (OTCD) and was participating in a clinical trial of a new gene therapy to use adenoviruses to ferry a corrected copy of the gene encoding OTCD into his liver cells. Unfortunately, four days after an infusion of the viruses, he died of acute respiratory distress syndrome and multiple organ failure, apparently caused by an overwhelming immune reaction to the large dose of adenoviruses he had been administered as part of the trial.

Although Gelsinger's death was part of a gene therapy trial, the tragedy also has ramifications for the new field of virotherapy. Gene therapy uses crippled versions of viruses such as adenovirus to introduce a new gene into cells; virotherapy employs actively replicating viruses (which may or may not contain added genes) to kill specific types of cells. Both, however, rely heavily on adenoviruses.

Gelsinger's autopsy showed that the engineered adenoviruses had spread to his spleen, lymph nodes and bone marrow, and an examination of his records revealed that his liver function was probably too impaired for him to be a volunteer in the trial. A number of scientists have also suggested that he might have mounted such an extreme immune reaction because he had previously been infected with a naturally occurring adenovirus.

Since Gelsinger's death, gene therapists and virotherapists alike have focused on refining adenoviruses to make them safer. But researchers are still unsure why Gelsinger reacted so violently to the adenoviral infusions: a second patient participating in the same clinical trial tolerated a similar dose of the viruses. And dozens of other people worldwide have been treated so far with adenoviruses with no serious side effects.

A National Institutes of Health report generated in the aftermath of Gelsinger's demise recommends that all participants in such clinical trials be monitored closely for toxic reactions before and after the infusion of therapeutic viruses. It also stipulates that volunteers be screened for any predisposing conditions that would increase their sensitivity for the viruses.

—D.M.N. and D.T.C.

genes that code for one or the other of these proteins become mutated or otherwise inactivated. Certain viruses, including adenovirus, interfere with the braking mechanisms of a normal cell by making proteins that stick to and inactivate Rb or p53. They do this because they can replicate only in cells that are preparing to divide.

Several research groups and biotechnology companies have engineered adenoviruses that fail to make the Rb or p53 blockers. Normal cells, which make these blockers, will stall the replication of these viruses by putting the brake on cell division. But these viruses will replicate in cells in which the Rb or p53 proteins are already disabled—cancer cells—and kill them. Curiel is planning clinical trials of the approach for ovarian cancer.

Researchers are also arming therapeutic viruses with genes that make the cells they infect uniquely susceptible to chemotherapy. The technique involves splicing into the viruses genes that encode enzymes that turn nontoxic precursors, or "prodrugs," into noxious chemotherapies. In one example, which was reported in 2002, André Lieber of the University of Washington and his co-workers designed adenoviruses to carry genes encoding the enzymes capable of converting innocuous prodrugs into the anticancer compounds camptothecin and 5-fluorouracil. The scientists engineered the viruses so that they could make the enzymes only in actively dividing cells, such as cancer cells. When they injected the viruses and the prodrugs into mice bearing implanted human colon

Selected Companies Involved in Virotherapy

Company	Headquarters	Virus	Diseases	Viral Modifications	Clinical Trial Status
BioVex	Abingdon, Oxfordshire, U.K.	Herpes simplex virus (HSV)	Breast cancer and melanoma	Carries the gene for granulocyte-macrophage colony stimulating factor, an immune system stimulant	Phase I/II
Cell Genesys	South San Francisco, Calif.	Adenovirus	Prostate cancer	Targeted to prostate cancer cells using prostate-specific promoters	Phase I/II
Crusade Laboratories	Glasgow	HSV	Glioma (brain cancer), head and neck cancer, melanoma	Has a gene deletion that restricts it to actively dividing cells such as cancers	Phase II for glioma and head and neck cancer; Phase I for melanoma
MediGene	Martinsried, Germany	HSV	Glioma and colon cancer that has spread (metastasized)	Harbors two gene deletions that prevent it from reproducing in normal cells	Phase II for glioma; Phase I for colon cancer metastases
Oncolytics Biotech	Calgary, Alberta, Canada	Reovirus	Prostate cancer and glioma	Able to replicate only in cancer cells bearing the activated oncogene *ras*	Phase II for prostate cancer; Phase I/II for glioma

Note: Phase I tests are designed to evaluate safety in small numbers of patients. Phases II and III are intended to determine the appropriate dose and efficacy, respectively.

or cervical cancer cells, they found that the viruses reproduced and spread in the tumors.

Such "smart" virotherapies are the vanguard of the future. But physicians will also need to track the activity of virotherapies in a patient's body to best assess how well the strategies are working and refine them further. Virotherapists are now teaming with radiologists to establish novel imaging technologies to easily measure how effectively a given virotherapy is replicating.

The imaging strategies involve inserting a gene that governs the production of a tracer molecule into a virus or virus-infected cell. The tracer can be either a fluorescent protein that can be observed directly or one that binds readily to the radionuclides used in standard radiological imaging techniques. The fluorescent protein might work best for cancers that are accessible by an endoscope, such as cancers of the larynx. Physicians could peer into the endoscope and see exactly where the viruses—and therefore, cancer cells—are by looking for fluorescence. So far the approach has worked best with viruses that do not kill cells, however. Nevertheless, we are convinced that such sophisticated imaging technologies will enable scientists to draw more meaningful conclusions from future clinical trials of virotherapy.

In 1995 gene therapy pioneer W. French Anderson of the University of Southern California School of Medicine predicted in [*Scientific American*] that "by 2000 . . . early versions of injectable vectors that target specific cells will be in clinical trials." These trials indeed began on schedule, as well as some he could not have envisioned then. We envision a substantial role for viruses—that is, *therapeutic* viruses—in 21st-century medicine.

The Authors

DIRK M. NETTELBECK and *DAVID T. CURIEL* began their collaboration at the Gene Therapy Center of the University of Alabama at Birmingham (UAB), where Curiel is director of the division of human gene therapy. Curiel, who holds an M.D. and a Ph.D., is the Jeanne and Anne Griffin Chair for Women's Cancer Research at UAB and a professor of gene therapy at the Free University of Amsterdam. Nettelbeck—who is now heading a research group focusing on virotherapy for malignant melanoma in the department of dermatology at the University of Erlangen-Nuremberg in Germany—was a molecular biologist and postdoctoral fellow of the German Research Association at the University of Alabama from 2000 to 2003. He received his Ph.D. in 2000 from Philipps University in Marburg, Germany, and was honored with a graduation award from the Novartis Foundation for Therapeutic Research.

More to Explore

"Gene Therapy: Designer Promoters for Tumour Targeting." D. M. Nettelbeck, V. Jérôme and R. Müller in *Trends in Genetics*, Vol. 16, pages 174–181; 2000.

"Replicative Adenoviruses for Cancer Therapy."
R. Alemany, C. Balagué and D. T. Curiel in *Nature Biotechnology*, Vol. 18, pages 723–727; 2000.

Vector Targeting for Therapeutic Gene Delivery. Edited by D. T. Curiel and J. T. Douglas. John Wiley & Sons, 2002.

"Cytolytic Viruses as Potential Anti-Cancer Agents." C. J. A. Ring in *Journal of General Virology*, Vol. 83, pages 491–502; 2002.

Gene therapy clinical trials database of *Journal of Gene Medicine*: www.wiley.com/legacy/wileychi/genmed/clinical/

American Society of Gene Therapy: www.asgt.org

6. "Hormone Hysteria?"

by Dennis Watkins

Hormone replacement therapy may not be so bad

Postmenopausal women have for decades relied on estrogen supplements to control the hot flashes, memory loss, osteoporosis and other ailments that can occur when their bodies no longer produce the compound. But hormone replacement therapy (HRT) is no longer considered the best way to treat menopause, ever since a report last year found that women receiving a certain type of HRT were at increased risk for dangerous side effects, such as breast cancer. Many health professionals have concluded that altering a woman's physiology will always increase risks over time. But a handful of respected scientists are calling for another look at HRT, arguing that not all therapies are created equal.

The largest blow to HRT appeared in the July 17, 2002, *Journal of the American Medical Association*. It presented important results of the Women's Health Initiative's long-term study of more than 16,000 women taking estrogen and a progesterone derivative. The study was halted prematurely, the authors reported, because too many women were encountering serious medical problems. "I believe that the drug we studied has more harms than benefits when used for the prevention of chronic diseases such as osteoporosis in generally healthy women," notes Jacques Rossouw, project officer of the initiative. In the past year a steady cascade of articles has enumerated all the higher risks that patients in the study experienced: an 81 percent increase in heart disease in the first year of therapy, a 24 percent increase in invasive breast cancer and a 31 percent increase in stroke. The therapy also doubled the risk of dementia. (A study of more than 800,000 women published in *Lancet* on August 9 also found an increased risk of breast cancer in postmenopausal women receiving a wide variety of HRT but noted that the risk of mortality from breast cancer related to HRT could not be determined.)

The essential ingredient of hormone replacement therapy is estrogen. Taken alone and without inter-ruption, however, estrogen causes cell division in the uterus, which in many women leads to uterine cancer. Women who have had hysterectomies can take estrogen by itself without fear of harmful side effects. (In fact, an estrogen-only arm of the Women's Health Initiative has continued because few participants have developed breast cancer.) For other women, though, the solution is to include a progestin, which blocks estrogen action in the uterus. Prempro, the Wyeth-manufactured drug used in the study, combines a cocktail of conjugated horse estrogens called Premarin with a synthetic derivative of progesterone called Provera, or medroxyprogesterone acetate. This pill, taken daily, was the most widely prescribed hormone replacement therapy drug in the U.S. when the initiative started during the 1990s.

For many scientists, a critical question yet remains: To what extent do the results of the initiative study apply to other forms of hormone replacement? "We cannot be sure whether other hormone combinations will have the same effects," Rossouw cautions, "but in my opinion we should assume they do until proven otherwise." But neuroendocrinologist Bruce S. McEwen of the Rockefeller University is unequivocally critical of the study: "I think that it borders on a tragedy that Premarin and Provera were chosen as the only HRT treatments."

A growing number of researchers believe that Provera is a poor substitute for progesterone. For example, medroxyprogesterone will bind in the breasts to progesterone receptors, which causes breast cells to divide after puberty and during the menstrual cycle, and also to glucocorticoid receptors, which causes cell division during pregnancy. This double-barreled assault on breast cells, explains C. Dominique Toran-Allerand, a developmental neurobiologist at Columbia University, probably led to the high rates of breast cancer in the study. "With Provera you are activating two receptors involved with cell division in the breast," she says, "and that's the culprit, not estrogen."

In addition, recent research shows that Provera interferes with estrogen's ability to prevent memory loss and dementia. "Estrogen is able to protect neurons against toxic assaults that are associated with

Alzheimer's disease," notes Roberta Diaz Brinton, a neuroscientist at the University of Southern California. Using in vitro studies of several types of progestin, she found that Provera—and no other progestin—blocks the mechanisms that allow estrogen to fight the brain's immune response to Alzheimer's. This immune response wears away at brain cells and causes them to leak neurotransmitters such as glutamate, which overloads and kills neurons. "It's basically as if someone were to open your mouth and shove down gallons" of soft drink, Brinton explains. "It's caustic, and you can't metabolize it enough."

Several researchers believe in the need for a study similar in scale to the Women's Health Initiative that tests hormones that more closely represent natural human hormones. Others suggest looking for better, more selective isotopes of the hormones. Until more research is completed, they agree, HRT deserves careful consideration.

Skeptic:
7. "What's the Harm?"
by Michael Shermer

Alternative medicine is not everything to gain and nothing to lose

After being poked, scanned, drugged and radiated, your doc tells you nothing more can be done to cure what ails you. Why not try an alternative healing modality? What's the harm?

I started thinking about this question in 1991, when my normally intelligent mother presented to a psychiatrist symptoms of cognitive confusion, emotional instability and memory loss. Within an hour it was determined that she was depressed. I didn't buy it. My mom was acting strangely, not depressed. I requested a second opinion from a neurologist.

A CT scan revealed an orange-size meningioma tumor. After its removal, my mom was back to her bright and cheery self—such a remarkably recuperative and pliable organ is the brain. Unfortunately, within a year my mom had two new tumors in her brain. Three more rounds of this cycle of surgical removal and tumor return, plus two doses of gamma knife radiation (pinpoint-accurate beams that destroy cancer cells), finally led to the dreaded prognosis: there was nothing more to be done.

What is a skeptic to do? An ideological commitment to science is one thing, but this was my mom! I turned to the literature, and with the help of our brilliant and humane oncologist, Avrum Bluming, determined that my mom should try an experimental treatment, mifepristone, a synthetic antiprogestin better known as RU-486, the "morning after" contraception drug. A small-sample study suggested that it might retard the growth of tumors. It didn't work for my mom. She was dying. There was nothing to lose in trying alternative cancer treatments, right? Wrong.

The choice is not between scientific medicine that doesn't work and alternative medicine that might work. Instead there is only scientific medicine that has been tested and everything else ("alternative" or "complementary" medicine) that has not been tested. A few reliable authorities test and review the evidence for some of the claims—notably Stephen Barrett's Quackwatch (www.quackwatch.org), William Jarvis's National Council against Health Fraud (www.ncahf.org), and Wallace Sampson's journal *The Scientific Review of Alternative Medicine.*

Most alternatives, however, slip under the scientific peer-review radar. This is why it is alarming that, according to the American Medical Association, the number of visits to alternative practitioners exceeds visits to traditional medical doctors; the amount of money spent on herbal medicines and nutrition therapy accounts for more than half of all out-of-pocket expenses to physicians; and, most disturbingly, 60 percent of patients who undergo alternative treatments do not report that information to their physician—a serious, and even potentially fatal, problem if herbs and medicines are inappropriately mixed.

For example, the September 17 issue of the *Journal of the American Medical Association* reported the results of a study on St. John's wort. The herb, derived from a blooming *Hypericum perforatum* plant and hugely popular as an alternative elixir (to the tune of millions of dollars annually), can significantly impair the effectiveness of dozens of medications, including those used to treat high blood pressure, cardiac arrhythmias, high cholesterol, cancer, pain and depression. The study's authors show that St. John's wort affects the liver enzyme cytochrome P450 3A4, essential to metabolizing at least half of all prescription drugs, thereby speeding up the breakdown process and shortchanging patients of their lifesaving medications.

But there is a deeper problem with the use of alternatives whose benefits have not been proved. All of us are limited to a few score years in which to enjoy meaningful life and love. Time is precious and fleeting. Given the choice of spending the next couple months schlepping my mother around the country on a wild goose chase versus spending the time together, my dad and I decided on the latter. She died a few months later, on September 2, 2000, three years ago to the day I penned this column.

Medicine is miraculous, but in the end, life ultimately turns on the love of the people who matter most. It is for those relationships, especially, that we should apply the ancient medical principle *Primum non nocere*— first, do no harm.

The Author

Michael Shermer is publisher of *Skeptic* (www.skeptic.com) and author of *How We Believe* and *In Darwin's Shadow*.

"Quiet Celebrity: Interview with B. Judah Folkman"

by Sergio Pistoi and Chiara Palmerini

The renowned medical researcher reflects on the promise of anti-angiogenesis drugs

The life of Judah Folkman took an unexpected turn one morning in May 1998. That day, a front-page article in the *New York Times* announced that Folkman, a professor at the Harvard Medical School in Boston, had discovered two natural compounds, angiostatin and endostatin, that dramatically shrunk tumors in mice by cutting the cancer's blood supply. Along the story was a quote from Nobel laureate James Watson: "Judah is going to cure cancer in two years." Watson eventually backed off, but the media frenzy had already exploded worldwide, transforming Folkman into a reluctant hero in the fight against cancer.

Folkman's reputation in the medical world was well established long before he hit the headlines. The son of a rabbi, he was a student when he developed the first implantable atrio-ventricular pacemaker in the 1950s. Later, he pioneered the first implantable polymers to obtain slow drug releasing. At the age of 34, when he became the youngest professor of surgery to be hired at the Harvard Medical School, he was already studying ways to block the formation of new blood vessels—a process called angiogenesis—to stop tumor growth. His ideas, initially met with skepticism by oncologists, are today the basis for an area of research that is attracting enormous interest. At least 20 compounds with an effect on angiogenesis are now being tested in humans for a range of pathologies that include cancer, heart disease and vision loss. But the premature hype continues to generate disproportioned hopes among the press, the public and the stock market. Recently, we met Folkman in his laboratory at the Children's Hospital in Boston to ask about his work and the progress of clinical trials on endostatin and angiostatin. —*Sergio Pistoi and Chiara Palmerini*

What makes anti-angiogenesis drugs a promising strategy in cancer therapies?

Many experiments showed that tumor growth and metastasis are angiogenesis-dependent. Tumors cannot grow unless they recruit their own private blood supply. That is why microvascular endothelial cells [the cells lining capillaries], which are essential for new blood vessel growth, have become an important target in cancer therapy. Antiangiogenic compounds do not attack the tumor cells directly, as chemotherapies do. Instead they turn endothelial cells off, so they won't make new blood vessels, and the tumor will eventually stop growing. The effect of angiostatin and endostatin is tumor-specific. So you have very few, if any, adverse effects on the organism. Targeting endothelial cells has some advantages: these cells are genetically stable, meaning that they do not mutate. In contrast, tumor cells tend to mutate and in this way they often become drug-resistant. Therefore, development of acquired drug resistance, which is common with chemotherapy, is less likely with angiogenesis inhibitors. Moreover, each endothelial cell can support up to 100 tumor cells; that means that by knocking out just few endothelial cells you have an effect on hundreds of tumor cells.

What impact did the sudden celebrity have on your daily work?

At the beginning I felt an enormous pressure. Patients were calling at all times and many flew to Boston. We hired three people just to answer the patients' and media's queries around the clock. [The news] raised expectations and demand for angiogenesis inhibitors before these drugs had completed testing in clinical trials. On the other hand, there are many patients alive today because they were treated with antiangiogenic drugs: thalidomide for multiple myeloma or low-dose interferon alpha for giant cell bone tumors or for angioblastomas. For any new type of therapy, there is always a dilemma about when to inform the public. If it's too early, then physicians are besieged by calls from patients for drugs that cannot be obtained. If too late, then critics say that hope was destroyed for patients with advanced disease. Our own research work was temporarily impacted because of many phone calls, but in the long run the effect was minimal.

The first tests in humans with endostatin began two years ago. What are the results so far?

The rules of clinical trials for endostatin are the same that the FDA sets for any other cancer drug. In the phase one of the trial you are only allowed to start with very few patients, for which any other option has failed, slowly increasing the dose in order to test the drug's safety. All phase I studied have shown that both endostatin and angiostatin are very well tolerated and have virtually no side effects. This is the most exciting thing about these drugs. On average a patient cannot stay on chemotherapy for more than six weeks, because either there are too many side effects or the tumor escapes [becomes resistant to the treatment]. So far, no patient has been reported to [have to] stop endostatin because of adverse reactions.

Furthermore, there were some patients whose disease became stable, and they regained their energy and weight. In few patients, there was also a slow tumor regression. [Results were reported in May at the meeting of American Society of Clinical Oncology and in the *Journal of Clinical Oncology*, September 2002]. Last spring endostatin moved to phase II to test its efficacy in rare neuroendocrine tumors of the pancreas. [Other phase II trials started in May (endostatin for metastatic melanoma) and July (angiostatin and chemotherapy for non-small cell lung cancer).]

Still, these results are very far from the dramatic improvements that you observed in mice. Why is it so difficult to replicate the experiments in humans?

Well, first of all these [Phase I] experiments are primarily designed to test a drug's safety, not its efficacy. Then, when you experiment with mice you can increase the dose, give different drugs in combination, and choose on which tumors and at what stage you want to try them. With humans, of course, the rules are strict: you can only give a single drug to patients with very advanced tumors, starting at very low doses. For example, we found the most dramatic effects in mice when endostatin and angiostatin were used in combination, but the FDA will not allow to use both drugs together before the end of phase II, maybe early phase III [large-scale, with many human patients] of the trials. Moreover, we have evidence that the drugs would work better if given at an early stage of the tumor. Another complication is that each tumor puts out different amounts of angiogenic stimulators. Some breast cancers, for instance, make only one angiogenic factor while others make six. That means that you have to balance the dose against a specific tumor, as much as you would adjust the dose of insulin according to your blood sugar levels for diabetes. But this is not the way you do clinical trials. You can't start with the dose you think is effective for each patient: everyone has to stay on a fixed schedule. But we are beginning to learn that when the drugs are approved—I don't know how many years that will be—a physician won't just stay on the same dose no more than you do with penicillin.

After endostatin and angiostatin were first hailed as the miracle cure, now many say that they are not meeting the expectations. How do you feel about all the ups and downs of your work in the press?

I feel that these drugs are not much different than any drugs going through clinical trials. Expectations are not the same for everyone. For example, researchers may have different expectation than the public or the press. Suppose that you read the abstract of phase I endostatin trial saying that the drug has shown "linear pharmacokinetics." It is a very good finding for an early trial, because it means that blood levels of the drug directly correlated with increasing doses, as predicted. But the same report can be deceiving for the public. It's very hard for reporters to explain the many hurdles of clinical testing of any new drug and it's hard for the public to understand that, on average, most drugs take seven to 10 years to be approved. Expectations are also biased by decades of experience with classic chemotherapy. With chemotherapy you expect to see a fast tumor regression, because the drugs directly kill the cancer cells; but it doesn't work this way for angiogenesis inhibitors, which are designed to turn off the blood supply, so that the tumor gradually slows down and, eventually, stops growing.

Do you think that clinical trials for antiangiogenic drugs should follow different rules?

No. The current guidelines for clinical trials are based on determining safety and efficacy and are working well. However, we must not forget the differences between antiangiogenic therapy and conventional chemotherapy. Some definitions, for example, do not have the same value. One example is the term "stable disease." For conventional chemotherapy it usually means "failure," because it may not last long and may be accompanied by many side effects and a poor quality of life. In contrast, for antiangiogenic therapy, patients with stable disease have virtually no symptoms and there is less of a risk of drug resistance if they are treated for a long time. Some patients refer to this situation as "having cancer without disease." In this case, the term "stable disease" has a completely different meaning.

Are you involved in the clinical trials of endostatin and angiostatin?

Trials are being carried on at centers in Boston; Houston, Tex.; Madison, Wis.; and Amsterdam and Utrecht in the Netherlands under the supervision of experienced oncologists. I have not participated directly. However, our laboratory has helped to develop some of the blood tests that are being evaluated in these trials and I help oncologists to design the trials.

What are your expectations for the future of these drugs?
My vision is that without any major side effect or resistance these drugs could be used in combination with other drugs or radiation therapy virtually lifelong. For the long term, over the next five to 10 years, we can ask whether the risk of drug resistance and the harsh side effects of treating cancer can be reduced, and whether cancer can ever be converted to a chronic manageable disease like diabetes or heart disease.

The Authors

SERGIO PISTOI is a freelance science reporter based in Arezzo, Italy. He can be found at www.greedybrain.com

CHIARA PALMERINI is a staff science writer for the Italian weekly magazine *Panorama*.

Profile: "Dissident
9. or Don Quixote?"

by W. Wayt Gibbs

Challenging the HIV theory got virologist Peter H. Duesberg
all but excommunicated from the scientific orthodoxy.
Now he claims that science has got cancer all wrong

SENAGO, ITALY—Three centuries ago cardinals
seeking refuge from a plague in nearby Milan stayed
here at the Villa San Carlo Borromeo, a grand estate
surveying the village from its highest hill. The villa and
its inhabitants have fallen on harder times since. The
cracked plaster and faded paint on its high walls are
covered with modern art of dubious quality. Now it is
the private museum of Armando Verdiglione, a once
prominent psychoanalyst whose reputation was stained
when he was convicted in 1986 of swindling wealthy
patients. Today the villa is hosting refugees of a different
sort: scientific dissidents flown in by Verdiglione from
around the world to address an eclectic conference of
100-odd listeners.

At the other end of the dais from Verdiglione is Sam
Mhlongo, a former guerrilla fighter and prison-mate of
Nelson Mandela and now head of the department of
family medicine and primary health care at the Medical
University of Southern Africa near Pretoria. Mhlongo
has urged President Thabo Mbeki to question the near
universal belief that AIDS is epidemic in South Africa
and that HIV is its cause.

Between them sits Peter H. Duesberg, an American virologist who has also challenged that belief. Duesberg is now tilting at a different windmill, however. In a reedy voice clipped by a German accent, he explains why he believes the scientific establishment has spent two decades perfecting an utterly incorrect theory of how cancer arises.

It is an odd speaking engagement for a scientist who isolated the first cancer-causing gene from a virus at age 33, earned tenure at the University of California at Berkeley at 36 and was invited into the exclusive National Academy of Sciences at 49. Today many of his colleagues from those early efforts to map the genetic structure of retroviruses occupy the top of the field. Robert A. Weinberg has a huge lab at the Whitehead Institute for Biology in Cambridge, Mass., with 20 research assistants, a multimillion-dollar budget and a National Medal of Science to hang in his office. David Baltimore got a Nobel Prize and now presides over the California Institute of Technology.

"I could have played the game and basked in the glory" of early success, Duesberg says, and he is probably right. But instead he broke ranks and bruised egos. And so, 10 days before attending this eccentric symposium, Duesberg had to dash off a desperate letter to Abraham Katz, one of the handful of rich philanthropists who have been his sole source of funding since he was cut off from all the normal channels five years ago.

"We're down to our last $45,000," the 64-year-old Duesberg confides glumly as we stand in the dark courtyard of the villa. Katz, whose wife suffers from leukemia, is his final hope; if this grant doesn't come through, Duesberg will have to cut loose his two assistants, close his lab at Berkeley and move to Germany. That is where he was born to two doctors, where he worked through a Ph.D. in chemistry and where he says he still has an open invitation to teach at the University of Heidelberg.

Leaving the U.S., if it comes to that, would thus close the loop on a roller coaster of a career. Although his ascendance is clear enough, it is hard to say exactly when his fall from grace began. Several weeks later as we talk in his small lab—one fifth the size of the facilities he once had—he hands me a paper he published in 1983. "This is the one that started it all," he says.

The paper is not, as I expect, his now infamous 1988 article in *Science* provocatively entitled "HIV Is Not the Cause of AIDS." Nor is it any of the several dozen articles and letters he published in peer-reviewed journals over the next 10 years arguing that the link between HIV and AIDS is a mirage, an artifact of sloppy epidemiology that has lumped together different

Peter H. Duesberg: Shunned Scientist

- His theory that HIV does not cause AIDS, outlined at **duesberg.com**, is rebutted at **www.niaid.nih.gov/spotlight/hiv00/**
- Twice married, he has one five-year-old son and three grown daughters. When not in the lab, he likes to roller-skate.
- "Surely 5 percent of the funds for science could be set aside for work on fringe theories that could be revolutionary."

diseases with disparate causes just because the sufferers have all been exposed to what he calls "a harmless passenger virus."

Although these dissenting theories of AIDS did not originate with Duesberg, he soon became their champion—and thus the target of derision for those who feared that disagreement among scientists could confuse the public and endanger its health. When Mbeki, after consulting with Duesberg and other AIDS experts, told the International AIDS Conference last year that he felt "we could not blame everything on a single virus," more than 5,000 scientists and physicians felt it necessary to sign the Durban Declaration, devoutly affirming their belief that HIV is the one true cause of AIDS.

Duesberg's arguments ultimately converted no more than a tiny minority of scientists to his view that "the various AIDS diseases are brought on by the long-term consumption of recreational drugs and anti-HIV drugs, such as the DNA chain terminator AZT, which is prescribed to prevent or treat AIDS." Or, as he puts it more bluntly in Milan, in rich countries it is the toxicity of the very drugs that are prescribed to save HIV-infected people that kills them.

The hypothesis has never been tested directly, although Duesberg claims it could be done ethically by comparing 3,000 HIV-positive army recruits with 3,000 HIV-negative recruits matched for disease and drug use. And so his idea has died as most failed theories do, never fully disproved but convincingly rebutted—in this case by a 40-page treatise from the National Institute for Allergic and Immune Disease—and ultimately ignored by nearly everyone working in the field.

But Duesberg didn't even know AIDS existed in 1983, when he wrote the paper that he says first marked him as a troublemaker. The title seems innocuous: "Retroviral Transforming Genes in Normal Cells?" But in Duesberg papers the question mark often signals that he is about to yank on the loose threads of a popular theory. This time the theory concerned cancer.

He and others had shown that when certain retroviruses insinuate their genes into the cells of mice, the cells turn malignant. Weinberg, Baltimore and others in the field speculated that perhaps similar genes, which they called "proto-oncogenes," lie dormant in the human genome, like time bombs that turn on only if a random mutation flips some sort of genetic switch. This hypothesis spawned a cottage industry to search for oncogenes, so-called tumor suppressor genes and, most recently, cancer "predisposition" genes.

As two decades passed, human genes with sequences similar to the viral oncogenes were found, and support for this story of cancer's origin solidified. "If you were to poll researchers, I'd guess 95 percent would say that the accumulation of mutations [to key genes] causes cancer," says Cristoph Lengauer, an oncologist at Johns Hopkins University.

But the story also grew steadily more complicated—and, to Duesberg, less convincing. Scientists expected

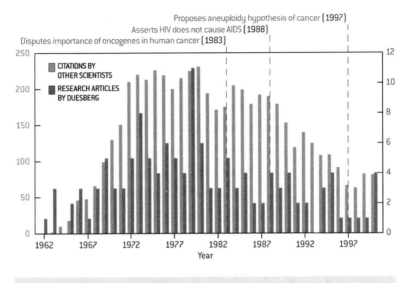

ROLLER-COASTER CAREER of Peter H. Duesberg is traced by the rate at which he has published research articles and the rate at which other scientists have cited his work.

to find some combination of oncogenes and tumor suppressor genes that are always mutated, at least in certain forms of cancer. They did not. Instead the number of putative cancer genes has leaped into the dozens, experiments have shown that different cells in the same malignancy often contain different mutations, and no clear pattern perfectly matches the supposed cause to actual human disease. Cells taken from patients' tumors typically translate their mutant genes into a mere trickle of protein, in contrast to the flood of mutated protein churning in cells transformed by a virus.

Beginning with his 1983 paper, Duesberg has also picked at theoretical weak spots in the orthodox view.

Some tumors are caused by asbestos and other carcinogens that are chemically incapable of mutating specific genes, he points out. Mice genetically engineered to lack tumor suppressor genes and to overexpress oncogenes should all develop cancer in infancy—but they don't. Given the measured rate of spontaneous mutations and the number of cells in the human body, the average person should harbor 100,000 cancer cells if even one dominant oncogene existed in the genome, Duesberg calculated in a paper last year. But if simultaneous mutations to three genes were required, then only one in 100 billion people would ever acquire cancer.

In 1997 Duesberg published what he thought was a better hypothesis. There is one characteristic common to almost every malignant tumor ever studied: nearly all the cancerous cells in it have abnormal chromosomes. In advanced cancers the cells often have two or three times the normal complement of 46 chromosomes. In new tumors the gross number may be normal, but closer examination usually reveals that parts of the chromosomes are duplicated and misplaced.

German biologist Theodor Boveri noted this so-called aneuploidy of tumor cells almost a century ago and suggested that it could be the cause of cancer. But that idea lost traction when no one could find a particular pattern of aneuploidy that correlated with malignancy, except in chronic myelogenous leukemia, which is not a true cancer because it doesn't spread from the blood to other parts of the body.

Recently, however, Duesberg and a few other scientists analyzed aneuploidy more closely and argued that it can explain many of the mysteries of cancer better than the current dogma can. Their alternative story begins when a carcinogen interferes with a dividing cell, causing it to produce daughter cells with unbalanced chromosomes. These aneuploid cells usually die of their deformities. If the damage is minor, however, they may survive yet become genetically unstable, so that the chromosomes are altered further in the next cell division. The cells in tumors thus show a variety of mutations to the genes and the chromosomes.

Because each chromosome hosts thousands of genes, aneuploidy creates massive genetic chaos inside the cell. "The cell becomes essentially a whole new species unto itself," Duesberg says. Any new "species" of cell is extremely unlikely to do better in the body than a native human cell—and that may explain why tumors take so long to develop even after intense exposure to a carcinogen, he argues. The aneuploid cells must go through many divisions, evolving at each one, before they hit on a combination that can grow more or less uncontrollably anywhere in the body.

So far Duesberg has only a scattering of experimental evidence to support his hypothesis. In 1998 he showed that there is a roughly 50-50 chance that a highly aneuploid human cancer cell will gain or lose a chromosome each time it divides. Last December he reported that aneuploid hamster cells quickly developed resistance to multiple drugs—a hallmark of cancer—whereas normal cells from the same culture did not.

But it isn't easy to do experiments when every one of his last 22 grant proposals to nonprivate funding agencies was rejected, he says. Although Duesberg maintained a facade of defiance in Milan, he acknowledged in a moment of fatigue that "it is depressing that even private foundations are unwilling to fund research that has high risk but high potential payoff."

His mood had lifted somewhat by May, when I visited his lab. A letter from Abraham Katz tacked to the door stated that his request was approved: he would be getting $100,000, enough to keep the lab running for another nine months.

It seems unlikely that nine months will be enough to persuade other researchers to take his aneuploidy hypothesis seriously. But it is possible. Numerous papers in major journals this year have pointed out the importance of "chromosome instability," a synonymous phrase, in cancer formation. Lengauer and Bert Vogelstein, also at Johns Hopkins, have been particularly active in promoting the idea that aneuploidy—which Lengauer insists must be a consequence of gene mutations—may be a necessary step for any tumor to progress.

Is Duesberg now willing to lay down his lance and play within the rules of polite scientific society? He recognizes that his combative stance in the HIV debate came across as arrogant. "With AIDS, I was asking for it a bit," he concedes. "At the time, I thought I was invulnerable." The experience may have tempered his ego, although he still mentions the Nobel Prize four times in a three-hour interview. Duesberg himself is pessimistic that he will ever be welcomed back into the club. "When you are out of the orthodoxy," he says softly, "they don't recall you."

Web Sites

Due to the changing nature of Internet links, Rosen Publishing has developed an online list of Web sites related to the subject of this book. This site is updated regularly. Please use this link to access the list:

http://www.rosenlinks.com/saces/taca

For Further Reading

American Institute for Cancer Research. *Stopping Cancer Before It Starts: The American Institute for Cancer Research's Program for Cancer Prevention*. New York, NY: St. Martin's Press, 2000.

Benowitz, Steven I. *Cancer* (Diseases and People). Berkeley Heights, NJ: Enslow Publishers, 1999.

Cooke, Robert. *Dr. Folkman's War: Angiogenesis and the Struggle to Defeat Cancer*. New York, NY: Random House, 2001.

Longe, Jacqueline L. *The Gale Encyclopedia of Cancer: A Guide to Cancer and Its Treatments*, 2nd ed. Farmington Hills, MI: Thomson Gale, 2005.

Mooney, Belinda. *Cancer* (Current Controversies). Farmington Hills, MI: Greenhaven Press, 2006.

Panno, Joseph, Ph.D. *Cancer: The Role of Genes, Lifestyle & Environment* (New Biology). New York, NY: Facts on File, Inc., 2004.

Ruzic, Neil, and David Ruzic. *Racing to a Cure: A Cancer Victim Refuses Chemotherapy and Finds Tomorrow's Cures in Today's Scientific Laboratories*. Urbana, IL: University of Illinois Press, 2006.

Silverstein, Alvin & Virginia, and Laura Silverstein Nunn. *Cancer: Conquering a Deadly Disease* (Twenty-First Century Medical Library). Minneapolis, MN: Lerner Publishing Group, 2006.

Sompayrac, Lauren. *How Cancer Works*. Sudbury, MA: Jones and Bartlett Publishers, 2004.

Waldholz, Michael. *Curing Cancer: The Story of the Men and Women Unlocking the Secrets of Our Deadliest Illness*. New York, NY: Touchstone Books, 1999.

Weinberg, Robert A. *One Renegade Cell: How Cancer Begins*. New York, NY: Basic Books, 1999.

Wyborny, Sheila. *Cancer Treatments* (Science on the Edge). Farmington Hills, MI: Blackbirch Press, 2005.

Index

International Congress of
   Ophthalmology, 64
ischemia, 30, 36

J

John Hopkins University
   School of Medicine, 12,
   16, 49, 63, 80, 108, 112
*Journal of the American Medical
   Association*, 88, 94
Journal of Clinical Oncology, 99
*Journal of the National Cancer
   Institute*, 59

L

Lancet, 89
Langerhans, Paul, 41, 42
Lengauer, Christopher, 16, 17,
   18, 21, 108, 112
leukemia, 11, 21, 54, 70,
   71, 106
Loeb, Lawrence A., 15, 21
Ludwig Cancer Institute, 46
lung cancer, 9, 59, 61, 99
lupus, 41, 50
lymph nodes, 44, 51

M

macrophages, 43
major histocompatibility
   complex (MHC), 44
malfunction, 15
malignant, 4, 6, 7, 9, 11, 13,
   16, 33
Massachusetts Institute of
   Technology (MIT), 6
"master" genes, 16, 17, 18, 21
medroxyprogesterone acetate, 89

melanoma, 46, 47, 59, 61,
   80, 99
metalloproteinase inhibitors, 28
metastases, 9, 12, 16, 20, 27,
   29, 79, 99
Merix Bioscience, 51
microbes, 46, 51
monocytes, 43
Murphy's Law, 5
mutant-gene theory, 11, 12

N

National Cancer Institute, 20,
   46, 59
National Council Against
   Health Fraud, 93
National Institutes of Health, 30
New York Times, 29, 96

O

oncogenes, 5, 10, 12, 14, 18,
   20, 108–110
oncologists, 5, 93, 97, 102, 108
ovarian cancer, 79, 83

P

papillary thyroid cancer, 12
pathologists, 37
peripheral tolerance, 50
pharmacologists, 60
photocoagulation, 62
photodynamic therapy (PDT),
   54, 55, 56, 59, 61, 64, 66,
   67, 71
polyps, 17
porphyria, 53–64, 66–67, 69–72
precancerous, 11
preclinical studies, 35